Italian Rustic

Italian Rustic

HOW TO BRING TUSCAN CHARM
INTO YOUR HOME

ELIZABETH HELMAN MINCHILLI

with
DOMENICO MINCHILLI

Photographs by
SIMON McBRIDE

Published by Artisan
A Division of Workman Publishing Company, Inc.
225 Varick Street
New York, NY 10014-4381
www.artisanbooks.com

Library of Congress Cataloging-in-Publication Data
Helman-Minchilli, Elizabeth.
Italian rustic: how to bring Tuscan charm into your home / Elizabeth Helman Minchilli
with Domenico Minchilli; photographs by Simon McBride.
        p. cm.
ISBN 978-1-57965-364-4
1. Farmhouses—Italy, Central. 2. Architecture, Domestic—Italian influences.
I. Minchilli, Domenico. II. McBride, Simon. III. Title.
NA8210.I7H46 2009
728'.60945—dc22   2009004413

Design by Susan E. Baldaserini

Printed in China
First printing, October 2009

10 9 8 7 6 5 4 3 2 1

THIS BOOK IS DEDICATED TO

Barbara Wood, Ursula Helman, and Rosa Minchilli,
the women who taught me how to make a house into a home with style,
and warmth, through cooking and entertaining—part of the recipe
that informs my work and life every day.

CONTENTS

PREFACE

Building an Italian Home

Eight years ago, in *Restoring a Home in Italy,* I told the stories of twenty-two homeowners, who shared their experiences about restoring buildings in Italy. Since its publication, both my husband, Domenico, an Italian-born architect, and I have received letters, e-mails, and telephone calls from as far away as Seattle, Santiago, and Oslo, asking us for advice. The questions went beyond the usual searches for fabrics or couches. People were hungry to know how terra-cotta tiles were laid down or how fireplaces were built. They wanted to incorporate these building techniques and traditions into their own homes, even those outside Italy.

While everyone is fascinated with living *la bella vita,* not everyone can make it to Tuscany. However, many people do want to incorporate Italian touches into their homes. This is what convinced us to compile this book, *Italian Rustic.* In researching Italian architecture, we looked at traditions that go back centuries and found that most of them are still alive today, especially in the rural Italian regions of Umbria and Tuscany. Indeed, many of the elements of Italian construction haven't changed much over generations. More important, we discovered that almost anyone, anywhere, can weave these elements into a design plan.

Italian Rustic a will work for you whether you are building a new house or simply redoing one room. You can read this book as a blueprint to a way of building, or simply pick and choose elements that work for you. Although you could use *Italian Rustic* to build from scratch, this is a book we hope will be useful for anyone wanting to infuse a bit of Italy into his or her life. Whether you desire Italian windows and shutters or just want your walls to look like they've been weathered by the Mediterranean sun, you will find the information you need to achieve an Italian rustic—style home within these pages.

Previous spread: *The salon of Dan Blagg and Francesco Bianchini's apartment in Todi, Umbria, was completely restored. The ceiling, hand-painted by Francesco, was inspired by decorations in the neo-classical Villa Mandri, outside Florence.* **Opposite:** *Begun in the eighteenth century as a formal villa, Palazzo Terranova remained unfinished for more than two centuries. After being used for many years by shepherds to shelter their flock, the palazzo was restored in 1997 and now functions as a luxurious boutique hotel.*

INTRODUCTION

What Is an Italian Home?

When we romanticize about Italy, we wax poetic about the warm, magical light, which gives even the air a rosy glow. We fall in love with the handmade, tactile quality of everything from a leather purse to a mouthwatering plate of fettuccine—each element crafted by hand and unique. Meanwhile, in Italian architecture, the sun-drenched colors and handwrought detail of Italy come together perfectly in rustic details such as stone walls and terra-cotta tile. Equally seductive are planks of honey-hued wood, cut by hand and polished by time.

This book focuses on the building methods of the rural regions of Umbria and Tuscany in central Italy. The rolling hills here are dotted with cypresses and vineyards in what is a quintessential Italian landscape. Built of stone, with a terra-cotta roof, the Tuscan or Umbrian farmhouse is what many of us dream of when we picture an Italian home.

Umbrian and Tuscan Italian farmhouses share many characteristics. Almost always constructed on two levels, these simple buildings were originally lived in by farmers and their families. The first floor was devoted to the workings of the farm, providing storage for equipment and—most important—shelter for the animals. Horses, cows, chickens, and rabbits were in rooms that were very roughly finished, with bare dirt floors and unplastered stone walls. Entry was gained through a large double door, handcrafted of wood. Once the doors were open, the doorway was usually the only source of light, since there were rarely any other windows on this floor.

An external stone staircase reached the living quarters on the second floor. The flight of steps ended at a small landing, which was usually covered by an overhanging roof that provided some shelter from the elements. The home was divided into several spaces, including a central room with a hearth. Not just a kitchen—although all the cooking went on here—this was the gathering place of the family. Electricity and plumbing came very late, if at all, and for many years the only source of heat was a large open fireplace, which was the heart of the home. As families grew, new wings were added, but each had a separate entrance, although the buildings were

The courtyard at Chiarentana, in Tuscany, is dominated by massive stone and terra-cotta staircases, each leading to a private apartment. The building dates to the fourteenth century and was recently restored by Donata Origo, who lives in the former castle and rents out apartments to visitors.

connected structurally. The final result was often village-like in appearance, with separate staircases leading to each family's home, varied rooflines and small chimneys signaling each separate family's residence.

Although farmers inhabited the houses, they were usually owned by wealthy landowners under a system known as *mezzadria.* In exchange for a portion of their crops, farmers were allowed a place to live in what was essentially a feudal system. After the system was dismantled in the 1960s, these houses were gradually abandoned, as the farmers left for cities to find more profitable work. And so the homes began to crumble, with roofs caving in and walls tumbling down. By the early seventies, abandoned farmhouses were almost being given away. For a few thousand dollars, farmers, as well as cash-strapped aristocracy, were more than happy to unload these neglected buildings onto Americans and British, as well as city-dwelling Italians in search of a bucolic way of life. And so began the newest chapter in the life of these homes.

The building techniques explored in *Italian Rustic* are twofold. One is a direct result of the history of the central Italian farmhouse itself. The other is a newer experience, the farmhouse's second life as a restored country home. Even though the original stone walls and terra-cotta roofs of Umbria and Tuscany were the attraction of this type of building, they had to be adapted to modern living.

In the following pages we will explore the history of Umbrian and Tuscan farmhouses as well as the unique solutions that today's owners, architects, and designers have devised to update the homes for modern life. In some cases, they have turned literal ruins into warm and inviting spaces. In *Italian Rustic* we will explore those strategies: how to create a kitchen where cows used to live, how to keep a house warm and insulated while still using terra-cotta tiles for the roof, and how to incorporate new rooms—such as kitchens and bathrooms—while still maintaining the original spirit of the Italian farmhouse. These modern solutions, developed on Italian soil, are the ones that we can apply when adapting an existing home or even building a new home, far from Italy.

Since many of the rustic techniques have not changed for centuries, this book will delve into tradition and visit the artisans who keep these traditions alive. The homes we visit in the hills of Tuscany and Umbria show innovative solutions to the challenges presented when bringing ancient homes into the twenty-first century. The elements we have photographed—floors, doors, fireplaces, and more—offer ways that you can bring these pieces of Italian living into your own home.

Much of the book is focused on very specific Italian building techniques and traditions, such as building a stone wall or laying a terra-cotta floor. For homeowners lucky enough to be able to build from scratch and source traditional materials and artisans, this information will prove invaluable. For others, who would like to impart the texture and feeling of *casa rustica* into their homes, understanding the nuts and bolts of tradition will enable them to choose alternative methods that are as close to authentic as possible. If you can't build a floor from the ground up, you can at least lay down tile *all'italiana.* And if building a sustaining stone wall is beyond your budget, perhaps a small retaining wall in the garden is the answer. Whatever your level of commitment, this book will allow you the freedom—and the knowledge—to choose which traditions work for you and bring them into your own home.

An artful display of black-eyed Susans sits on the table on the terrace of a home in Umbria.

CHAPTER ONE

STONE WALLS

Imagine a farmhouse in the Italian countryside, and what often comes to mind first are lichen-covered, weathered stone walls. Rough-hewn and massive walls are essential to the look of rustic Italian architecture. But stones are not merely a decorative element, tacked on to a façade. They are literally the building blocks of rustic architecture. Before you can apply this ancient look to your own home, it is essential to understand how this material has been used for centuries to craft the farmhouses that dot the fields and valleys of central Italy. Even if you aren't planning on building stone walls from scratch, it is still possible to capture some of their allure.

*Previous spread: Kate Ganz and Daniel Belin built this guesthouse, which they call The Barn, on their property in Umbria. The building was constructed using building materials salvaged from other ruins. A mixture of stones and bricks were used to create the walls, and the design even includes a "ghost" window, which appears as if it had been bricked over centuries ago. **Opposite:** Ganz and Belin's home was originally a farmhouse. The building retains its original footprint, but the addition of several windows and the chimneys, which dot the roof, shows some modern adaptations. **Above:** A handcrafted wrought-iron railing leads up the outdoor staircase of a home in Tuscany.*

THE TRADITION OF STONE

One of the reasons stone was used for farmhouses was its minimal expense. In rural areas, when fields were plowed, stones came to the surface every season and were a no-cost building material. The stones were carefully collected, sorted according to size, and used to build retaining walls, property borders, and walls for homes and stables.

The walls of an ancient farmhouse consist of whole rocks. Many attempts to replicate this ancient process fail from the start because the stone is used as a veneer rather than as a building material. Although a stone veneer may look like a stone wall, it certainly won't feel like one unless it has the visual depth of a true stone wall. To recapture the true spirit of the original architecture, we must understand why and how these walls are built.

A row of flat stones and bricks forms the top of this stone wall in Umbria. This last row is thinner, but slightly wider so that the overhanging edge protects the wall below it from the elements.

BUILDING NOTES: A TRADITIONAL STONE WALL

The dimensions of Italian walls are partly defined by the material itself: stone. The walls usually range from a minimum thickness of 20 inches (50 cm) in domestic architecture to a more massive width of 40 to 60 inches (100–150 cm) in castles, palaces, and other large buildings. Stone walls are heavy and require a sturdy foundation. This foundation, which is also known as the foot, is usually twice the width of the wall itself. The wall's width is determined by the average size of the stones used, usually 10 to 12 inches (25–30 cm). Since two rows of stones are used, the average thickness of a common stone wall is about 20 to 24 inches (50–60 cm). So the foot, or foundation, is wider to give a stable supporting base.

Once the foundation is laid down, the wall itself is built up. While the foundation can be up to four stones deep, the sustaining wall is usually two stones deep. Traditionally, the material used to set the stone was a mixture of lime and sand, or even soil that had been strained of organic elements. Today the mixture is usually made of water, cement, and rough sand.

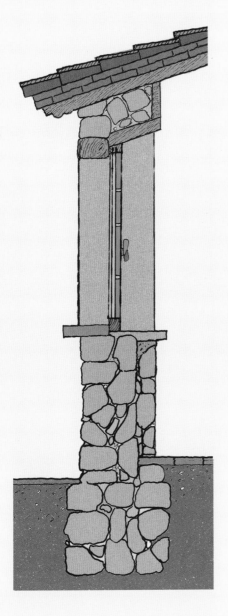

This cross-section of an external wall shows its construction from foundation to roof, with a window inserted.

BRICK

In some areas of Italy, brick is preferred to stone as a building material—especially where clay is more plentiful. The heyday of brick manufacturing was the nineteenth century. In some areas, such as the countryside around Perugia in Umbria, or Siena in Tuscany, semi-industrialized kilns sprang up to meet demand. The bricks produced found their way into farmhouse architecture, particularly as a material used for the walls of newer additions to older stone houses. For instance, when we decided to add on a bath to our stone house in Umbria, we could have used stone. But for a more authentic and eclectic look we opted for walls in locally made brick. Similarly, the upper story of Kate Ganz and Dan Belin's home in Umbria, which was probably added at a later date, is of brick while the lower level is of stone. Also note that in old stone walls, pieces of brick traditionally were used to fill in the small gaps between stones or to level out a flat surface for the next row of stones.

While this wall was mainly built of stone, bricks were used for newer additions, such as the edges of the window openings. A terra-cotta cornice delineates the original structure from the newer section above it.

BUILDING A STONE WALL TODAY

Outside of Italy, stone isn't always available or even affordable to use as a structural building material, and skilled stonemasons aren't that easy to find. But elements that can be incorporated into any Italian farmhouse-style home are the appearance of stone and the solid feeling that a stone wall imparts.

Creating a Stone Veneer

Even in Italy the use of stone as a construction material isn't always possible. Contractors often suggest a faster way of building, using hollow clay brick faced by a veneer of stone. The bricks are standard size (10 by 20 or 12 by 24 inches, 25 x 50 or 30 x 60 cm) and are set upon a foundation. The stone facing is applied to the exterior in a layer of one row of stones and attached every few feet to the brick wall through a series of metal ties. The wall then consists of a row of bricks just under a foot (25–30 cm) thick and a row of stones not less than 10 inches (25 cm) thick. This final wall measures about 20 to 24 inches (50–60 cm) thick.

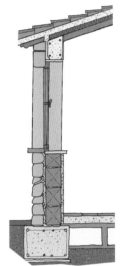

Creating Depth

One of the most important elements in Italian wall construction is the sense of massiveness and depth. From the outside, this feeling is imparted by the material itself: large, heavy stones. But it is from within the building that the importance of thick walls, and their almost sculptural effect, really comes into play.

Because elements such as doors and windows are set *into* the wall, the depth of the wall becomes part of the architectural vocabulary. The niche created by a thick wall is three-dimensional, creating shadows that are important elements of Italian-style homes. While it may be easier to create the look of an Italian wall, with different finishes inside and out, the feel of the wall is just as important. Whatever construction technique you choose—drywall, brick, or even stone—keep in mind the final thickness of the wall as a design element integral to your finished room.

*Opposite: One of the defining characteristics of a stone farmhouse in Italy is the thickness of the walls. Nowhere is this more apparent than in the openings created for windows. Here, in this castle in Umbria, the ancient walls are thick enough to allow for two window seats. **Overleaf:** At Palazzolaccio, in Tuscany, the ancient courtyard walls display a mix of stone, brick, and terra-cotta—added over the centuries.*

THE FINISHING DETAILS

Grout

Cement holds the stones together in wall construction, but the final layer of grouting in between the stones takes on an aesthetic role as well. Applied to the surface of the finished wall, the grout fills in gaps between the rough stones. One of the mistakes made when building a stone wall from scratch today, or even restoring an old wall, is to apply the grouting too carefully. The grouting in stone walls in farmhouses was usually applied with a trowel, and almost thrown against the stone. It was roughly spread with the edge of the trowel to cover much of the exposed stone. In other words, it looks quite rough—not perfect.

*Left and right: Masons in Italy use whatever materials are available to create a stone wall. Large stones anchor the construction, while smaller stones and pieces of brick and tile fill in gaps. The final grouting is applied very roughly. **Opposite:** Stone walls are often plastered to protect them from the elements. Here at Casaccia, a home on the La Foce estate in Tuscany, the large farmhouse has been plastered and painted a bright, sunny yellow.*

Stucco

Exposed stone walls may be romantic and picturesque, but they certainly aren't the only Italian option. Even when stone was used in Italian farmhouses, it was often covered by a layer of stucco, or *intonaco,* on the exterior surface. Plaster gives a stone wall an added layer of sophistication. While simple farmhouse walls were often made of exposed stone, the landowners' houses, or villas, were more likely to be covered in plaster, which gave a more elegant appearance as well as added protection against the elements. In any stone wall, the weakest point is the grouting between the stones, where moisture can seep in and easily degrade the bond, eventually showing up as humid spots on the interior surface. A layer of stucco, about one inch thick, helps protect the wall, and requires no painting. The stucco itself is made up of cement and fine sand (or marble dust). Color choices often depended on local traditions and wealth. Adding ground tile, brick dust, or other pigments directly to the mix can create an aged and worn feeling to the plaster.

Portals, Window Frames, and Corners

While roughly dressed stones make up the bulk of walls, when it comes to the edges, the details are usually more refined. When a wall ends—whether it is at a window or a door opening or at a corner—the edges must be strong enough to support the stresses of the rupture. Windows and doorways are often reinforced by large slabs of local stone, as well as by sills below. A less expensive alternative is to use bricks to form the edges, especially at the corners of buildings. The contrast of bright red bricks and honey-colored stone was used to create a wonderfully textured doorframe at a home outside of Orvieto, Umbria, owned by a British couple, Carolyn and James Twist (see page 106).

Left: *The stone walls at this villa in Umbria have been plastered over to provide an extra layer of protection and an elegant, finished effect.* **Center:** *Masons choose stones carefully to fit into the overall scheme of the wall. The corners are particularly challenging, since the edges must be squared off. When a new window is opened in an ancient wall, the masons insert terra-cotta bricks along the edges.* **Right:** *Flat, horizontal bands of stones are interspersed with terra-cotta bricks and tiles to make up this wall in Umbria.*

STONEMASONS

Although stones are obviously formed by nature, skilled artisans select them. Since a wall must be a certain size to support a building, masons choose stones that together create a structurally stable base. To an untrained eye, all stones may look the same, but a stonemason can easily pick out the best ones. A prerequisite is that the flat side of a stone be of a certain size so that it can be placed into the wall horizontally to create a series of flat layers. Look carefully at a stone wall: you will notice that it isn't just a random sequence of stones but a systematic pattern, with horizontal bands of similarly sized stones that run its full length.

The best stones for building have a flatter side or two. But regardless of the original shape, the stones usually have to be adjusted by the stonemason, with a sort of hammer, called a malenpeggio. This double-sided tool is shaped like a pick on one side and a small ax on the other. Stones that are used at corners or wall openings require even more intervention since the angles must be perfectly perpendicular.

BRINGING IT HOME: STONE WALLS

Not everyone can afford to use stone as a construction material. Building in stone can be costly, and qualified stonemasons hard to find. Fortunately, there has recently been a resurgence of stoneworking both in the United States and abroad. Contact groups such as the UK-based Dry Stone Walling Association (see resources, page 222) for a referral to a qualified artisan.

Even if you're not building an entire stone-walled house from scratch, there are less elaborate ways to incorporate stonework into your home. Don't be afraid to combine stone with other building materials, such as brick, when creating an addition. This is the method used in Italy, where most farmhouses are eclectic, organic creations that have been added to over centuries.

In Italy, stones are often used outside the home, adding rustic charm to the garden and other landscape elements. Try using stone for retaining walls, or as a low border for a flower or herb bed. Another option is to use stones for outdoor paving. Large slabs of local stone can be used for paths or paving to great effect.

*Above: At Zingoni, the Mianis' home in Tuscany, a massive retaining wall serves to support the covered terrace adjacent to the house. **Opposite:** The Mianis used large slabs of local stone at their other home, Casellacce, to pave the terrace.*

CHAPTER TWO

INTERIOR WALL FINISHES

Anyone who has been to Italy brings back memories of palaces, villas, churches, and museums adorned with elaborate frescoes. While most of us won't be decorating our living rooms with scenes from the Sistine Chapel, we can borrow from and incorporate into our homes Italy's glorious tradition of wall finishes. Whether the rough feel of plaster, the smooth finish of stucco, or the intricate designs of frescoes, the walls of an Italian home evoke a way of life. What's more, this thin layer of plaster and paint is one of the easiest ways to add Italian rustic charm to a room. The key to these lovely finishes often lies below the surface: traditional methods of rustic Italian wall preparation ensure the vibrancy and texture of that last layer of color.

Previous spread and above: The lime-based paints used throughout the Fattoria di San Martino, in Tuscany, are mixed using natural pigments. Opposite: The kitchen at Gonzola, a farmhouse on the La Foce estate in Tuscany, has been lime-washed a stunning shade of blue, following a local belief that blue keeps flies away.

BUILDING UP TO A FINISH

Italian rustic farmhouses are usually built of large, roughly dressed blocks of local stone layered with cement to form thick walls. The interior sides of these walls are treated with a special base. While most modern homes in the United States start out with relatively smooth surfaces, such as plasterboard, in Italy the goal is to smooth the rough and bumpy stone surfaces to a level base. The process consists of two layers: the *intonaco;* and the *velo,* or *colletta.*

The First Layer: *Intonaco*

As with many Italian building elements, the first layer of plaster goes by many names. The most common are *rinzaffo* and *intonaco.* Traditionally this first layer is applied by the stonemason, who mixes local sand with *calce,* or lime, a method that has been gaining in popularity as a more natural alternative to cement. The mason carefully mixes the sand and lime with water to a creamy consistency, just thick enough so it doesn't drip.

The mason then uses a *cazzuola* (trowel) to pick up some of the freshly mixed plaster and throw it against the wall, with a soft *thwump!* The force of the throw is actually very important, since it allows the plaster to make its way deep into the crevices between the irregular stones. Using the same tool, the plaster is smoothed down and pushed into cracks, evening out the bumpy surface. Eventually the stone is covered, and a more or less pristine surface is ready for the next layer.

The Second Layer: *Colletta*

The second layer has an almost infinite number of variations, going from barely covered plaster to highly decorated frescoes that are almost glass smooth. In between are finishes that require very specific skills and materials. In Umbria this is called *colletta* and derives from the word *colla,* or glue, since the layer is thin and sticky like glue. In slightly more poetic Tuscany, it is called *velo,* like a veil, since it is that thin. Regardless of the term, the aim is to apply a thinner, more refined layer to the rough *intonaco,* or plaster, below. This second layer, like the first, is made up of a mixture of lime, or cement, and very fine sand and water, but mixed to a thinner consistency. It, too, is applied with a specialized type of trowel called *l'americana.*

THE FINAL LAYER

The last layer applied to the plaster covering the stones is very thin, only 2 to 4 millimeters (about ⅒ inch). Varying degrees of smoothness can be achieved; the final choice is in part an aesthetic decision, and in part a financial one. The smoother the wall, the more labor involved. And for a perfectly smooth finish, in which extra tools such as metal guides are used, the cost can soar.

Left: At Fattoria di San Martino in Montepulciano, the owners used very thin washes of pigmented lime to coat the walls, doors, and built-in bench. This faded, almost pastel look lends an authentically weathered feel to this restored farmhouse. **Right:** *At Zingoni, Ilaria Miani chose much more intense shades to highlight a doorway opening, lending a crisp and modern feeling to this restored home in Tuscany.*

At Loggiato, a small country inn in Tuscany, a small bath was created. Though the room is simple in design, the walls were lime-washed with a very untraditional shade of shocking pink.

Intonaco Civile

Intonaco civile, or civil plaster, is one of the final layers. It is applied both to protect the wall and to create a visually pleasing surface. The sand used is fine, and the thickness of this layer is usually no more than ¹⁄₁₀ inch (3 mm). Traditionally this final layer is also tinted with color so that no further painting is necessary.

Decorative Plasters: *Stucco Romano* and *Stucco Veneziano*

One of the most popular ways to incorporate an Italian decorative element into your home is to use a specialized plaster technique such as *stucco Romano* or *Veneziano.* The gleaming surfaces of Italian decorative plasters date back to Roman times. The classic recipe includes dust from ground *pozzolana,* a type of volcanic sand, which enables the finish to reach an almost glasslike shine. Another key ingredient is slaked lime putty, which is mixed with stone dust, usually marble or quartz, then colored with pigment. The skills used to develop these finishes were perfected in the sixteenth and seventeenth centuries in and around Venice, which is where Venetian plaster got its name. Today a wide range of firms produce premade mixtures, using both organic ingredients and acrylic binders, which make the technique easier to execute.

APPLYING COLOR

Abandoned farmhouses in Italy often boast some of the most beautifully mottled pastel walls. The pale hues ripple across the rough layers of plaster, weathered by years of use, kitchen smoke, and sometimes exposure to the elements. At the other end of the spectrum are painting traditions that have more in common with palaces and villas.

Farmhouse Color

Generally, in farmhouses, after the *intonaco* is finished, the paint is applied. This is done *a calce*, or with a lime-based paint, to which pigment gets added. Lime-based paints are commonly used because they are thought to be more attuned to the vagaries of humidity, letting the wall "breathe" rather than locking in the humidity. In Italy it is still traditional to use this formula—rather than newer latex-based paints—for ceilings and in more humid rooms, such as bathrooms and cellars.

In the traditional Italian farmhouse, color represented an extra cost: the more pigment, the bigger the expense. This consideration resulted in a palette that is primarily pastel, in tones of blue, green, and pink, since pale shades require less pigment. Because the part of the walls that received the most wear and tear was the area near the floor, where mops and brooms would sweep up dirt and water, a painted *battiscopa,* or baseboard, was traditionally applied. This was often no more than a 4- to 6-inch (10- to 15-cm) strip of a more intense color than that applied to the walls, but it could also be a contrasting color.

The Classical Wall

If your taste goes back centuries, then true fresco, or *affresco,* can provide rich patterns and colors that are literally part of the fabric of the wall. The word *affresco* comes from *fresco,* or fresh. The technique, used by such artists as Michelangelo and Raphael, dates back to the Renaissance. Each day a section of plaster would be applied to the wall, and while the fresco was still wet, or fresh, the pigments would be put on. Since the pigments would adhere only to wet plaster, which would dry in twenty-four hours, only small sections were applied every day. Add to this the fact that the pigments changed colors as they melded with the plaster and dried and one begins to understand the mastery involved in this technique.

A modern version, *finto fresco,* or fake fresco, is less labor-intensive. Like true fresco, it uses pure pigments, but these are mixed with *grassello di calce,* or lime plaster, to give texture to the colors. As in true fresco, the pigments reveal themselves only once they are dry, but at least the artist can work on a dry wall, with more freedom, and skip the daily application of wet plaster.

If even this method is too complicated, an easier version exists that allows still greater freedom. In this case, the wall is prepared and the plaster left to dry. It is then sanded down to give it a rough surface. The design is applied with either acrylics or simple wall paint. You can distress the wall further, to give it an aged look, by roughing up the surface with sandpaper. There are also many products, such as glazes and varnishes, that can add a transparent coat of color to age the painting further.

Opposite: Above: Dan Blagg and Francesco Bianchini re-created the look of a traditional casettone *ceiling by painting trompe l'oeil paneled squares inspired by the design of a ceiling in a Tuscan villa. The larger beams are decorated with an eighteenth-century motif, while the frieze that runs around the entire room is Pompeian. Francesco used tempera paints with natural pigments to create the decorations. Below: The natural pigments used to tint the lime-based paint at Fattoria di San Martino give a mottled, aged look to the brightly colored walls throughout the building.*

EXPOSED STONE

The walls of an Italian farmhouse are made from carefully chosen stones, in hues of gray and sand. It is tempting to leave these artisanal creations completely exposed, even indoors. But the original tenants of farmhouses almost never left stone walls bare inside their living quarters. On the ground floor, where the animals lived, the walls were usually roughly treated. But upstairs, where the family resided, the stone walls were always covered with a layer of plaster so they would be easier to keep clean. This layer of plaster and sometimes color was not just a decorative decision. It kept humidity, dirt, and bugs at bay.

Today's homeowners are often tempted to keep at least the downstairs walls intact, with huge blocks of sculptured stone dominating the room. "I can understand the appeal of these walls, since they were handcrafted and tell part of the history of the house," says Domenico. "But at the same time, most people don't realize that the stones, while beautiful, are dark, and reflect almost no light. A room with four stone walls can be incredibly dim and oppressive."

An alternative is to keep one wall made of stone, while plastering and painting the others. Domenico advises that a single stone wall, such as this one in a bedroom of a house in Umbria, is enough to create a cozy effect.

In the Twists' Umbrian home, Domenico, who was the architect, took advantage of an existing stone wall, leaving it exposed to great effect in the ground-floor guest bedroom.

BRINGING IT HOME: INTERIOR WALL FINISHES

Although Italian-style wall finishes often look simple, achieving them almost always involves a high level of mastery and professional skill. Finding the correct materials and applying them with proper technique is not easy, and the best results come from trained artisans.

Luckily, today there are many decorative painters highly skilled in this craft. An architect, designer, or general contractor will be able to point you in the right direction. There are also national groups, such as the Colorado-based Professional Decorative Painters Association, that offer a directory of their membership.

In terms of expense, the more elaborate your design, the higher your cost. A highly polished stucco Veneziano finish can mean a serious investment. However, many rustic, lime-based finishes on the market cost much less (see resources, page 221).

Any of the painting techniques described in this chapter can be applied to the smooth surfaces of drywall, rather than a stone wall base, but there will always be something missing. Even if you can't see the building blocks of a stone or brick wall beneath the layer of fresco in an Italian home, the very subtle rippling of the surface is always present. If you are starting with a smooth wall, you may want to consider adding a slightly bumpy, hand-applied layer of plaster at the end to simulate the classic look.

*Above: The wall finishes throughout Palazzo Terranova are completely new, since the original eighteenth-century building had never been completed. The palette, however, was inspired by the richly colored frescos of Renaissance painter Piero della Francesca. **Opposite:** At her home Casellacce, in Tuscany, Ilaria Miani chose a muted palette for one of the guest suites.*

CHAPTER THREE

FLOORS

Whether tile or wood, the floors in an Italian farmhouse are essential to the authenticity of their look. A great deal of craftsmanship goes into the manufacture and installation of Italian terra-cotta tile and hand-cut wood floors. We will also explore decorative options such as tinted cement and majolica tiles. Often used in modern farmhouse restorations, these are easy elements to add a bit of *vita italiana* to any room.

*Previous spread: Hand-made, square terra-cotta tiles cover the kitchen floor at Casellacce, in Tuscany. The tiles are set at a 45-degree angle to the wall, and the resulting diagonal lines make the room appear larger than it actually is. **Opposite:** At Loggiato, in Tuscany, wide and narrow planks of hand-cut oak provide a warm floor. **Above:** Salvaged roof tiles from a farmhouse are used here as flooring.*

TERRA-COTTA TILES

When we lay down a handmade terra-cotta tile in our own home, we are following a tradition that goes back thousands of years. Recently, while digging foundations for a new home Domenico designed in Umbria, workers unearthed a terra-cotta tile that retained the first-century A.D. stamp from a Roman kiln. Except for the date, there was not much difference between this two-thousand-year-old tile and the ones that are still being made today. The Tuscan and Umbrian towns that became known for making tiles in the sixteenth century—Impruneta, Castelviscardo, and Deruta—are still major suppliers. And luckily not much has changed in this essentially ancient process. Although some of the steps, such as the stirring and mixing, have been mechanized, the essential crafting of the tiles and the drying methods remain unchanged.

Above: The owners of Fattoria di San Martino reused the original ceiling tiles as flooring. They left them unsanded and traces of the original ceiling paint still show through the wax. ***Opposite: Left:*** One of the most traditional designs for laying down rectangular terra-cotta tiles is the fishtail pattern. ***Center:*** A diagonal pattern often lends a sense of movement while a horizontal pattern (**right**) works well in rooms with right angles.

Choosing Your Tiles

Terra-cotta tile works in almost any room. The soft, neutral color fits into almost any scheme, and once the tile is installed, its upkeep is relatively simple. The hard surface is easy to clean, making terra-cotta a good choice for rooms with a lot of wear and tear, such as the kitchen and bathroom.

Even though the process of making terra-cotta tiles is the same from town to town, there is room for creativity. The color of terra-cotta tile reflects the hue of the clay from the region where it was made. In fact, the Italian word *terracotta* means "baked earth." Tiles made near Impruneta, in Tuscany, usually have a dark, russet tone that reflects the high level of iron in the clay. Around Castelviscardo, in Umbria, the clay is closer in tone to peach. Each *forno,* or tile maker, also has its own closely guarded secrets regarding temperature control and drying, which influence the final color as well.

One of the most exciting aspects of choosing your tiles is the chance to develop a pattern for each room. Although there are a limited number of tile shapes, the patterns they can form are almost limitless. The most common shape is the simple rectangle, which measures 6 by 12 inches (15 x 30 cm). Other shapes include octagons and squares, as well as smaller tiles that allow you to develop more complicated, almost carpetlike patterns.

One final aspect of tiles is the level of smoothness. Tiles fresh out of the kiln have a rough texture, which some people prefer for their rustic appeal. However, most people choose to smooth them out, at least to a certain degree. Tile can be hand-sanded at the kiln, which lends a more irregular, and so more authentic, look to the finished floor. An alternative is to grind the tiles down once they have been installed, which creates a much more even surface.

RIGHT OR WRONG: CHOOSE YOUR SIDE

When tile makers press the wet clay into the molds, the side facing downward is smooth and the side facing upward is rough and wavy, bearing the imprints of hands and tools. Although the smooth side is meant to be installed facing up, more and more homeowners are opting for the rougher side. But this choice drives Italian contractors insane (why would *anyone* intentionally choose a rough surface?). "We really liked the handmade feeling of the 'wrong' side of the tiles," says Carolyn Twist, whose home in Umbria is paved with tiles from nearby Castelviscardo. "You can sometimes see thumbprints or tool marks, and every so often we even get a paw print from a cat that must have walked over the tiles before they were quite dry!"

Installing Tile

TO GLUE OR NOT TO GLUE: With a traditional material like terra-cotta, it is tempting to follow time-honored installation methods. Masons soak the highly porous tiles in a basin of water overnight, and the next day they are set into a 2-inch (5 cm) screed—or base layer—made of sand, lime, and water. This technique has the advantage of allowing leeway for the slightly uneven thickness of the handmade tiles. A thick tile can be pressed deeper into the screed, while a thinner tile can float atop a thicker layer—ensuring an even surface even if the tiles themselves are

Above left: The factory stamp is clearly visible on this handmade tile, installed with the "wrong" side intentionally facing upward. Above right: Terra-cotta tiles are adhered with a thin layer of glue laid down atop a cement base. Opposite: Dan Blagg and Francesco Bianchini's home in Todi retains its original terra-cotta floors. Years of wear and wax have brought out the varied colors of the clay.

uneven. But it is a very wet process; between the overnight soak and the water to mix the screed, gallons of water are used, requiring a very long drying time. In the damp winter months, tile installed this way can take up to six weeks to dry completely. Even in the heat of summer, at least two weeks are needed to make sure the tiles are absolutely dry.

A more common technique these days is the use of tile glue. The glue is laid down in a very thin layer and the dry tiles set firmly into it. Although this method doesn't allow for much variation in the thickness of the tiles, it has the advantage of being much quicker. Since no water is used, drying takes just twenty-four hours.

PLACING YOUR TILES: Regardless of the pattern you choose, a decision common to all projects is the distance between the tiles. This may seem to be an almost inconsequential point, since we are talking about the difference of an eighth of an inch or so. But that small measure can make all the difference. Traditionally, tiles were laid down as close as possible. But since the tiles were irregular in size, there had to be some flexibility in grouting to make them line up in rows or in a repeatable pattern. Modern contractors, in the pursuit of speedy installation (and, frankly, because of a lack of skilled labor) tend to make the space between tiles wider. This speeds up the grouting process and provide greater tolerance for variations in tile size. Yet when the grouting is too wide, the tiles look like they are floating in a bed of cement rather than forming one perfect expanse of warm, glowing terra-cotta. The effect looks wrong even to the untrained eye. Although close positioning takes more time—and skill—it pays to set the tiles as close as possible.

GROUTING: Traditional grouting is a mixture of fine sand, lime, and water, sometimes tinted by the color of the local sand. These days, ground-up terra-cotta is often added to commercially bought cement (which is grayish) to tint it very slightly. Industrial grouting comes premixed in a huge palette of colors. Although it may be tempting to choose a color that matches the tiles you are using, traditional grouting has been neutral, with only a minimal tint. The best choice for an authentic look is a neutral off-white that will age naturally as the floor does. In other words, although a lot of thought should go into the grouting, in the end you don't want to notice it. In Laura Evans's home in Umbria, the contractor spent days mixing different amounts of ground-up tile into the premixed grout to achieve a color that, while warmer than plain grout, didn't look too pink either.

GROUTING TECHNIQUES

THE CLASSIC METHOD

Traditional grouting was quite liquid, and a small can with a spout was used to pour the material into place. As the worker poured, he would help the grouting penetrate the gaps with a small spatula, then gently smooth and wipe away the excess material with a rag.

THE MODERN METHOD

A faster way is to pour an excessive amount of grouting over the surface of the tiles. The liquid grout finds its way into the crevices, and the excess is then washed away. Modern contractors prefer wide gaps between the tiles to allow the grout to flow in easily.

CLEANING UP

No matter how your tiles are set and grouted, the floor must be thoroughly cleaned. Workers mix 30 percent muriatic acid with 70 percent water and pour the solution over the entire floor. The acid at this strength will quickly eat away any tiny particles of grouting that have remained on the tiles while leaving the tiles themselves unaffected. Abundant clear water is used to wash away both acid and excess grouting.

Hexagonal and square tiles look antique but are newly handmade by Fornace Giuliani. The irregular grouting widths contribute to the aged look.

Above: Terra-cotta tiles are installed in a fishbone pattern in Kate Ganz and Daniel Belin's connecting living rooms in Umbria. Each room has a double row of tiles running parallel to the walls, creating a carpetlike effect. *Opposite:* The deep red color of the terra-cotta tiles in a castle, in Umbria, was intensified with an application of a traditional red-tinted wax.

THE FINISH: Since terra-cotta is an extremely porous material, it is usually sealed to protect it from dirt and stains. But because of its ability to absorb humidity like a sponge, it must be perfectly dry before any finish is applied. If the tiles were laid down using cement (not glue) and a large quantity of wet grouting, the drying process can take several weeks to a month. This technique is obviously possible only when the house is under construction and no one is living there.

The finish of your tiles is a very personal choice. Americans Kate Ganz and Daniel Belin chose a traditional finish for the floors of the four farmhouses they have restored in Umbria. The contractor applied linseed oil several times, until the tiles were completely impregnated with the oil. Once the oil was completely absorbed, liquid beeswax was applied and the tiles were buffed to achieve a higher shine. Antonio Giorgini and his wife, Karin Lijftogt, the owners of Fattoria di San Martino, a farm inn outside of Montepulciano in Tuscany, go one step further in their use of authentic materials. "For the final coat I use beeswax from my own honeybees," explains Antonio. "Although it seems like a delicate material, it is actually quite protective. We usually reapply it about every three or four months. It has the added benefit of smelling heavenly!"

Although many people in Italy still use the traditional linseed oil–beeswax mixture, there are also modern, industrial products that can both seal and wax the floors. In the end, the effect is almost indistinguishable. That said, there is something about the rich perfume of linseed oil and warm beeswax that no modern product can imitate.

THE WARMTH OF WOOD

Where there is clay, there are tiles. And where there are trees, there is wood. Traditional building in Italy follows the motto "use what you have," and so it goes with flooring materials. Clay was abundant in southern and central Italy, and so a tradition of terra-cotta tiles developed. Farther north, in Lombardy, Piemonte, and the Aosta Valley, larger trees translated to wooden floors.

Pick Your Planks

There is a reason they are called hardwood floors. In Italy, the hardest local woods have always been chosen to stand up to the rough tread of shoes and boots. The most commonly available Italian woods are elm, chestnut, and oak. For our home in Umbria, we were lucky enough to buy a supply of perfectly aged cypress from Tuscany. In 1984, our friend Paolo, a farmer, had to cut down a century-old cypress on his property to avoid its toppling over from a crippling disease. By the time we laid down our floor, in 1993, the wide golden planks were aged perfectly, and they now fill our home with their heavenly, pitchy scent.

Another plus in buying our wood from Paolo was the traditional manner in which he sliced the trunk. Each plank was cut according to the circumference of the tree, with nothing going to waste. When we laid down the floor, we made sure that wide and narrow alternated with long and short to create a varied pattern that we never tire of looking at.

Modern flooring is often sold in standard sizes, which makes it easier to store and ship. The problem is that, when it is laid down, it gives a much more finished and polished look than the types of planks in rustic farmhouses. You might want to choose planks that differ in both width and length to achieve a more traditional look.

Another modern style of wood floor consists of planks that are finished with tongue-and-groove edges, so that when they are assembled the finished surface is extremely smooth and tight. You should avoid these prefinished planks if you want to achieve a rustic look. A better choice, which most closely captures the effect of hand-planed, irregular boards, would be straight-edged planks that, when nailed into place, produce a slightly uneven effect.

Wide planks of hand-cut pine were nailed down to form the floor at Fattoria di San Martino in Montepulciano.

BASEBOARDS

At Loggiato, in Tuscany, wide oak boards are used for the flooring. Following rustic tradition, the boards are laid down very close to the wall, without an added wooden baseboard. A painted band of deep peach is used instead. Even though terra-cotta or wooden baseboards are available in Italy, making it easier to clean the floors without splashing the walls, they are a recent invention and give a modern, inauthentic look to a finished room.

Finishing the Wood Floor

In farmhouses, wooden floors were often left untreated. In palaces or villas, wax was used, but it almost never reached a high shine. The finish was always slightly dull. We left our own cypress floor in Umbria untreated. Over the last fifteen years, it has slowly yellowed and aged.

But not all farmhouse floors were left untreated; where possible, a natural coating of oils and wax was applied. At Fattoria di San Marino, the wooden floors were treated with the same recipe used for terra-cotta floors. Linseed oil was slathered on and absorbed by the wood. Then beeswax was warmed to a liquid state and brushed on. After a day or so, when the wax had been completely absorbed and was cooled, it was buffed by hand.

Today products with acrylic components emulate the look of beeswax, are more permanent, and give more protection to the wood. The most durable of these are the polyurethane, solvent-based sealants (although they have an extremely strong odor and are not environmentally friendly). The newer water-based sealants are healthier and more environmentally friendly, albeit more expensive and not as durable.

Two Ways to Lay a Wood Floor

In traditional Italian farmhouses, the wooden floor planks were nailed directly to the beams supporting the ceiling below (see Building Notes: Floors, page 49). Although almost no one nails down floorboards directly to the supporting beams anymore, there is a springiness to nailed floors that is hard to give up. To achieve this look, smaller sticks of wood are set into a thin layer of concrete, about a foot (30 cm) apart. The wooden floor planks are then laid atop these sticks and nailed in place. This method has all the charm of the traditional method—such as squeaking, springing under the feet, and a general old-fashioned feeling. Yet it does away with the disadvantages of light and dirt going through the cracks to the floor below.

The modern option is to lay the floor with glue. The wooden floorboards are glued directly to the structural concrete. This method eliminates at least one step in the process but results in a floor that lacks the spring and give of an old-fashioned nailed floor. It has practical advantages, though. Wood planks that are glued down are generally thinner than those that are nailed, and so less expensive. Also, since there is no need for wooden slats to be inserted into a layer of concrete, the installation process is much faster and takes less space.

OTHER FLOOR OPTIONS

CEMENT

Cement, a material that in Italy dates to the 1940s, was originally used for storage areas, stables, or cellars. But today many homeowners are choosing tinted cement floors for everything from kitchens to living rooms. For instance, Kate Ganz and Daniel Belin chose waxed cement for some of the rooms in their house in Umbria because they thought it looked less formal than terra-cotta tile. "I also liked the idea that the smooth surface would reflect the light and bounce it around the room, which turned out to be very effective," says Ganz.

MAJOLICA TILES

Majolica tiles are terra-cotta tiles that have been painted with lead-based glazes and fired again, to fuse the pigments into a hard, glass-like surface. This costly material was rarely found in rustic farmhouses, where only the humblest elements were used. Today many people are drawn to the beautiful patterns and bright colors of majolica tiles. Majolica is rarely used for great expanses of floor as it once would have been employed in villas or palaces. Instead, it is being incorporated on a smaller scale, as a decorative accent. The tile's hard, impermeable surface makes it a natural choice for bathrooms or as a kitchen backsplash or countertop.

Above right: A polished concrete floor helps to keep this guest bedroom in Umbria cool in the summer.
Right: Salvaged nineteenth-century majolica tiles, from the south of Italy, are fairly easy to find. This brightly colored pattern is from Lacole, in Umbria.

Most rustic Italian homes have massive, hand-carved beams running across the ceilings. Although gorgeous to look at, these weighty, almost sculptural elements were functional, not decorative. Beams were designed to support the floor above the ceiling (be it wood or tile). Large beams, called *trave*, measure about 12 inches (30 cm) in diameter and span the room, from one supporting wall to the other. Smaller squared beams, called *correnti* or *travetti*, run perpendicular to these to create the surface that will support the floor above. In original Italian farmhouses, the flooring material was placed directly atop these smaller beams. This rustic method let dirt, light, and sound penetrate between the cracks. Today builders have several options for maintaining this authentic look while adding a bit of modern convenience.

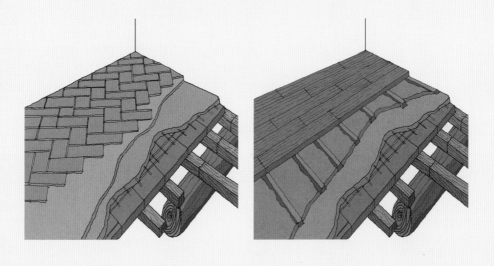

Left: *Many layers are involved in constructing a terra-cotta tile floor on a wood base. The ceiling of the room below would consist of that base, held up by wooden planks. The reinforced concrete between the wood and terra-cotta is hidden between the ceiling and floor.* **Right:** *Here, instead, wooden planks are used for the floor while terra-cotta tile is visible as the ceiling in the room below.*

TERRA-COTTA TILES | FORNACE GIULIANI

CASTELVISCARDO, UMBRIA

Fornace Giuliani has been crafting terra-cotta tiles from local clay for more than one hundred and twenty years, in this small town in Umbria, not far from Orvieto. "My grandfather started the business, and my father, Ernesto, and I still run it," says Massimiliano Giuliani. "I hope it will go on to the next generation, but my son is still in grade school, so it's hard to tell yet!" Like generations before them, the Giulianis get their material locally, from the dense, rich beds that have been supplying the trade since Etruscan times. The dry clay is mixed with water as needed.

1. *Fornace Giuliani stockpiles a mixture of local dry clay. The raw clay is mixed with water, then kneaded. Once ready to be used, it is loaded onto a cart and taken to the molding area.*

2. *A chunk of wet clay is cut and placed over the wooden frame, which rests on a workbench. After pressing the clay firmly into the mold, the tile maker levels off the tile with a roller.*

1.

2.

3. The tile maker carefully turns the still-wet tiles out of the molds and lays them on the ground, in huge warehouses, to dry. The length of the drying period depends on the season. In summer the tiles dry in a few days, but in winter they can take up to two weeks. Workers tend the tiles the entire time, turning them frequently, since even drying is crucial.

4. Workers carefully stack the dry tiles on metal pallets, which they wheel into an enormous kiln. The walls are made of earthen bricks, and the entire kiln is hermetically sealed while the tiles bake for about two days. The tiles remain in the kiln until they are completely cooled.

5. Workers sort and store the finished tiles, which are prepared for delivery. Tiles can be used as they come out of the kiln—rough but ready—or slightly ground down. Although terra-cotta tiles continue to be used locally, they are also shipped around the world.

3.

4.

5.

The choice of flooring in a home is usually approached in the earliest stages of the design. When laying a foundation, it's very important to consider the thickness of the material to be used. Will it be relatively thin wall-to-wall carpeting or much thicker tile? That said, with a bit of planning, almost any type of floor can be made to work. Just be sure your contractor knows what you have in mind before the foundation is laid.

If your heart is set on terra-cotta, a wide range of tile has become available in the United States (see resources, page 223). The most authentic, of course, are handmade terra-cotta tiles imported from Italy. If you are feeling adventurous, order directly from several manufacturers in Italy, specifying size, color, and finish. Alternatively, some American distributors carry a wide range of high-quality, handmade Italian tile. A more affordable alternative is handmade terra-cotta tile imported from China, South America, and Mexico. These tiles are of varying quality, but some are quite beautiful and should stand up to years of wear.

Finding a craftsman to lay terra-cotta tile should not be too difficult since, from a practical point of view, terra-cotta is not that different from any other type of tile installation. The trick to getting the right look is threefold: first, choose the right tiles; next, lay the tiles as close together as possible; finally, ensure that the finish is not overly shiny, using a natural linseed oil and wax for the finish if possible. If you feel that you want a stronger, more protective finish, choose one of the low-shine, synthetic finishes available on the market.

Hardwood floors are common throughout the world. To get an authentic Italian look, choose boards made from woods domestically common in Italy: oak, pine, and chestnut. An excellent choice is reclaimed planks offered through such companies as Pioneer Millworks, based in Farmington, New York. The mill's Settler's Plank Oak is made by resawing salvaged beams from old barns (see resources, page 324).

An easier alternative is to glue machine-cut boards in place. Though the look and feel are not as authentic, this type of wood flooring is widely available and affordable. If you choose it, try to find untreated wood, and provide the last layer of wax on your own. Most planks come pretreated with an acrylic sealant.

Salvaged terra-cotta tiles are piled high at Lacole. The varied textures and colors of antique tile are irresistible. Just know that the irregular thicknesses make them a challenge to install.

CHAPTER FOUR

CEILINGS

W alk into an Italian farmhouse, and you immediately notice the ceilings. These building blocks of construction are essential tools in almost any structure in Italy. Massive wooden beams, and alternate methods such as arches, not only hold up the building but also can provide a feeling of hand-hewn solidity that is at the heart of Italian rustic style. Even though today's construction methods, which include the use of reinforced concrete, mean that most homes won't need wooden beams for support, it is still possible to borrow from this tradition to impart the weight of Italian rusticity.

Previous spread: The vault in the dining room of Palazzo Terranova, in Umbria, was constructed during its renovation twelve years ago. The terra-cotta tiles are laid edge to edge, using a technique called volte a folio, *in which tiles are laid flat with their thin edges touching and gesso is used as mortar.* **Opposite:** *The owners of Locanda del Loggiato, in Bagno Vignoni, salvaged their home's original roof tiles, which are now supported by the original hand-carved oak beams.* **Above:** *Hand-made terracotta roof tiles rest atop* mezzane, *or cross beams, in this Umbrian ceiling.*

WOOD BEAMS

Characteristic among farmhouses in central Italy are the large, dark wooden beams that run across ceilings. Up to 12 inches (30 cm) in diameter, these loglike elements are sunk into the walls at either side. Traditionally, they had to be long enough to span the room, and thick enough to support the floor, or roof, above. While building codes in Italy today require the addition of reinforced concrete in the construction of floors, beams are still used as the main supports in rustic home construction.

Big Beams

Floors in rustic Italian homes were constructed of two layers of wooden beams, or *trave*. The main load was supported by huge, hand-carved beams, which spanned the shorter width of the usually rectangular room from one bearing wall to the other. The beams measured anywhere from 15 to 21 feet (4.5–6.5 m) long and about 10 to 12 inches (25–30 cm) in diameter, and were squared off roughly.

Small Beams

Smaller beams, called *travetti*, were then laid atop the larger beams perpendicularly. These beams were squared around the edges or sometimes left almost rounded. They spanned the space between the larger beams, and their diameter or width corresponded to the length they had to span: the larger the span, the thicker the beam. The distance between one small beam and the next was determined by the flooring material to be used above. When standard-size terra-cotta tiles were used, the beams were about 1 foot (30 cm) apart. If, instead, wooden planks were used, then the distance between the beams increased, as did the diameter of each beam.

While the ceiling of this Umbrian guesthouse looks antique, it is in fact new. Antique ceiling tiles, supported by hand-hewn oak beams, were sanded and treated for an aged look.

ALTERNATE SUPPORTS

As iconic as beams are in Italian rustic farmhouses, they are not the only traditional way to build a ceiling. Where large pieces of wood were unavailable, other methods developed, such as using tiles and bricks to build arches. And as the use of new materials—such as concrete and steel—became common, other methods evolved, including the use of reinforced concrete.

Arches

The most common type of arch used in rustic farmhouses is the brick groin vault. An extraordinarily beautiful example is in Kate Ganz and Daniel Belin's dining room in Umbria. Clay bricks are laid with their thick edges against one another to form what are essentially two intersecting barrel vaults. The thrust of the vault is concentrated along the groins and is supported at the four corners of the room.

Voltine

Another type of support, *voltine*, was developed in places where wooden beams were harder to obtain. Beams are used to span the room, and small arches are constructed to span the space between these beams. Since the arches were stronger than the timber system, fewer beams were needed. Eventually the wooden beams came to be replaced by steel beams, eliminating the need for wood entirely. A typical example is in Ilaria Miani's kitchen and living room in Palazzolaccio, one of seven homes this interior designer and her husband Giorgio have restored in Tuscany. Flat terra-cotta tiles were laid with the edges against one another and span the distance between the steel beams.

Opposite: In a dining room, a new brick groin vault supports the ceiling. To construct it, elaborate wooden scaffolding was built to support the arches. **Below:** *The vaulting in this antique Tuscan ceiling—in a room once used as an animal stall—was created using a system developed at the end of the nineteenth century. Using steel beams rather than wood ones allows for a larger ceiling expanse.*

Left: *In a guesthouse in Umbria, hand-finished oak beams support the roof and balcony loft.* **Right:** *Steel beams support terra-cotta tiles in a series of vaults, called* voltine, *at a home in Tuscany.*

Left: *The ceiling of a bedroom on the second floor of Fattoria San Martino, in Tuscany, reflects the steep pitch of the roof, which the massive beams support.* **Right:** *The entrance hall of a home in Umbria was created by taking out the original floor separating the first and second levels, thereby creating a double-height room. In lieu of windows, a skylight runs the length of the ceiling, flooding the stairs with natural light.*

CEILING FINISHES

Today many homeowners leave their wood or tile ceilings unadorned. They love the rich browns of the oak, elm, and chestnut beams and the warm hues of handmade terra-cotta tile. But historically, farmers who could afford a bit of elegance often sought to downplay these rustic and humble building elements by painting over the entire ceiling, including the beams and tiles.

"Although we appreciate the rough-hewn nature of the original beams today, the original tenants of these farmhouses tended to mask the 'natural' elements," explains Domenico. "When exploring farmhouses that are half in ruins, you often see entire ceilings not only whitewashed but painted pastel hues of green, pink, and blue. Our own fascination with exposed beams is a relatively recent thing."

Some modern owners still prefer this effect. In Casaccia, part of the large La Foce estate in Tuscany, the owners were lucky enough to be able to reuse many of the original beams and tiles in their restoration project. In one of the dozen small farmhouses that dot the property, the kitchen, living room, and bedrooms ceilings were whitewashed for a lighter effect.

In a new kitchen, the ceiling was constructed traditionally, with wooden beams and terra-cotta tiles, then painted white to provide a lighter and more luminous atmosphere.

BEAMS | NUCCIARELLI WOOD MILL

AMIATA, TUSCANY

The Nucciarelli wood mill is tucked into the hills of Tuscany, nestled amid the chestnut forests that supply the raw material they have been crafting into beams for half a century. Started by Valter Nucciarelli in 1957, the company is run today by his son, Rodolfo. "The wood that we work with is almost entirely local," says Rodolfo. "Mostly chestnut, which comes from the area directly around us. But also pine and oak, as well as Douglas fir, which was planted in this area in the 1930s and is only now ready to harvest."

The large trunks are bought from both private owners harvesting their own land and larger firms that grow these trees. The wood is then aged for anywhere from three or four months to three years. "The wood that is destined for carpentry use is cut up into boards and then aged. The beams, instead, are aged in their trunk form and then shaped." The entire aging process takes place in the open, a method that is becoming increasingly rare. Rodolfo notes, "Most mills use an artificial aging process, using ovens to dry the woods. We prefer this more natural method. It takes longer, of course, but the results are better."

Left: Chestnut trunks are left in the open air for the elements to age them. Right: A chestnut trunk is squared off for use as a supporting beam.

BRINGING IT HOME: CEILINGS

Beams were originally there for a reason: to hold up the roof and ceiling. Newer methods of construction, such as reinforced concrete, have eliminated the structural need for beams. Today many people try to imitate the look by applying strips of wood to their ceiling to mimic true structural beams. To avoid a blatantly fake look, search out hand-hewn, aged beams that look their part and measure the appropriate size to actually support the floor above.

Wood mills, a good source of planks for wood flooring, can usually special-order very large beams. In Italy, salvaged beams are often used, and their weathered charm lends texture to restorations. In the United States, specialized firms offer reclaimed timbers that can add an aged and massive feel (see resources, page 224). If you do use new wood, consider painting the entire ceiling, beams included (as they did at Casaccia on page 64). In Italy, this look is just as authentic as a white ceiling lined with dark wood beams.

In an Italian farmhouse, the average beam measures 12 inches (30 cm) in diameter. Beams hanging from the ceiling can take up quite a bit of headspace, so make sure that you have sufficient ceiling height before you get your heart set on beams. In addition, since beams must be sunk into the supporting wall to appear functional, a certain amount of construction must be planned ahead.

Above: Another option, used in this Tuscan kitchen, is to whitewash the tiles while leaving the beams in their natural state. Opposite: Massive chestnut beams bear the weight of the ceiling in this living room and support the floor above.

CHAPTER FIVE

ROOFS

Anyone who has driven through central Italy—or seen a film set in the rolling hills of Tuscany—is familiar with the warm rich tones of terra-cotta roofs. Undulating, curved tiles, weathered and rich with the mottling of lichen and the patina of time, form a multilayered tapestry. Rooflines are animated by different slopes, chimneys, and complicated systems—the result of centuries of additions and changes. As families grew, additions were built, and each new wing had a distinctive outline. If you are lucky enough to build from scratch, or just adding on a new room, consider embracing this visually haphazard approach. Even in an existing home, adding such details as a handcrafted chimney can add a touch of Italy to your home.

Previous spread: Installed two decades ago, during the restoration of this Umbrian roof, these terra-cotta roof tiles were industrially made, but have weathered and taken on the patina of age.
*Opposite: In this covered porch, massive chestnut beams hold up the terra-cotta roof. **Above:** A detail showing the traditional method of roof tile installation in which curved tiles are set atop handmade curved terra-cotta tiles—called* coppi—*placed on their backs (see page 80).*

ARCHITECTURAL UPS AND DOWNS

Even though new construction exists in Italy, most buildings are the result of decades, if not centuries, of creating additions to existing structures. While churches like St. Peter's in Rome took hundreds of years to finish, even simple farmhouses are never really "done." Original buildings were added on to, year after year, as the family grew and more space was needed. (Only recently have zoning laws restricted haphazard additions to homes.) Nowhere is this organic building plan more evident than in the roof profile. From the tower of a fortified castle in Umbria (page 76), the varied rooflines, heights, and slopes of the terra-cotta-covered roofs tell the story of floors added, buildings extended, and even a chapel and bell tower erected.

While I'm not suggesting that you take out an extended agreement with your contractor to come back every decade or so and add on to your home, you can certainly plan your house from scratch to imitate this varied and colorful profile. For example, Domenico made a new house in Chile come alive with a roofline that rose and ebbed, encompassing five different heights.

While building styles change from region to region in Italy, nowhere is the variation more evident than in roofing techniques and traditions. Italy today stretches from the northern Alps—with abundant rain and snow—to the dry regions of Sicily and Puglia. Roofs with a steep slope and highly resistant stone tiles let the rain and snow run off in the north, while flat, white, plastered roofs reflect the sun in the south, making them cooler. In between, in central Italy, are the roofs that we have come to think of as most Italian: the terra-cotta tops that dot the countryside.

Vintage terra-cotta tiles, salvaged from another building, were used in this farmhouse restoration in Tuscany. The varied colors of the clay tiles, coupled with the weathered surfaces, result in a warm and rich tapestry of texture and hue.

MATERIALS

Tile

When restoring old farmhouses in Italy, every effort is usually made to salvage the terra-cotta tile from the original structure. This is not just to save money but also because these tiles have been weathered by the sun and rain over decades, creating a look and feel almost impossible to replicate. Antique terra-cotta roof tiles are sometimes available from salvage yards.

A less expensive alternative is to use new terra-cotta tile. At the low end of the price range are industrially produced tiles. Uniform in both shape and color—usually a very dark reddish orange hue—these are affordable but bland.

In between vintage and industrial are handmade new tiles. Since they are also rougher in finish, and more porous, they will weather quickly to provide a mottled, rich color.

Coppi—or curved roof tiles—are sold at Lacole, in Umbria. Although these tiles all came from one farmhouse, they include newer, commercially made tile as well as older handmade ones.

Edges

Walk up to a house, and the first thing you see is the edge where the roof meets the wall. This seemingly small detail can make a huge difference in authenticity.

Even if you decide on the traditional beam-and-tile construction for your roof, you will need to add layers of structural concrete, weatherproofing, and insulation. In an old Italian farmhouse, one of the most delicate details traditionally was the tile overhang that perched over the roof's edge. With these extra layers, that edge can run up to 8 inches thick (20 cm) and can form an awkward and unsightly profile.

There are various solutions to this problem. The aim is to avoid a thick, visible layer of concrete. At Kate Ganz and Daniel Belin's house in Umbria, one solution was to use a double layer of horizontal floor tile at the edge to mask the cement.

Left: Roof restoration in Italian farmhouses means adding thick layers of reinforced concrete and insulation. To mask this layer of structural material, a triple layer of terra-cotta tiles has been added along the roof's edge. Right: The overhang of a roof provides a wall with protection from the elements.

CHIMNEYS

One of the least predictable and most creative aspects of roof design is the construction of chimneys. In Italy, these often perky and inventive structures pop up in seemingly random places atop the terra-cotta slopes of roofs. Even though they obviously correspond to the fireplaces below, they look like so many candles atop a terra-cotta cake.

*Opposite: A jaunty pair of brick and terra-cotta chimneys rises above the roof of this Umbrian villa nestled in a hidden valley between Tuscany and Perugia. **Above:** This new brick chimney was constructed during the restoration of a farmhouse in Umbria to accommodate a new fireplace below. **Overleaf:** Blackened by smoke, these chimneys in Tuscany were constructed of handmade, local brick.*

Structurally, the roof follows the same rules as those used for building a floor, only at an angle. Large beams, called *trave*, measuring 12 inches (30 cm) in diameter, span the length of the room, meeting at a perpendicular angle the beam that runs across the top at the uppermost point. Smaller beams, called *travetti* or *correnti*, run perpendicular to this.

The exact angle of the roof varies from region to region: in the south, where there is less rain, the roofs were flat, and in the north, the angle was steeper to allow the rain and snow to run off. In central Italy, the slope is usually about 17 degrees, which allows for the amount of precipitation in that region to run off.

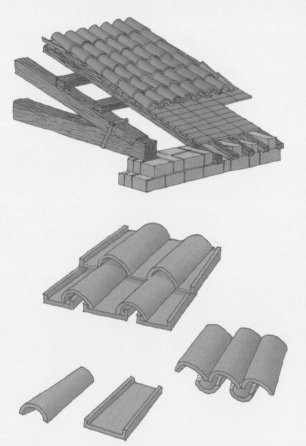

In traditional building, the tiles were set directly onto the smaller beams, weighted down every so often with stones. Today's builders add several more layers. On top of the smaller beams, a 2-inch (5-cm) layer of reinforced concrete is laid down. This is required by new building codes and more evenly distributes the weight of the roof over the supporting walls. After a 2-inch (5-cm) layer of insulation, a waterproofing layer, made of asphalt, is put on top. Finally, the roof tiles are laid down.

Roof tiles rest directly upon wooden beams in traditional roof construction. There are two types of traditional roof tiles. Each method uses coppi, *or curved tiles. In the top illustration the* coppi *rest upon flat, lipped, tiles called* tegole romane, *or embrici. Below,* coppi *are paired with* coppi, *each fitting into each other.*

TERRA-COTTA CHIMNEYS | FRATELLI BERTI

RIPABIANCA, UMBRIA

In Umbria, where clay is plentiful and skill is high, builders have been using terra-cotta chimneys and other decorative elements to top their roofs for centuries. "We are one of the few that still produce terra-cotta chimneys," says Remo Berti, who always keeps some in stock at his family's business. "When you are driving through Umbria, it's pretty common to see not only terra-cotta chimneys but also terra-cotta parts of bell towers and even finials on top of villas and churches. Recently when they were restoring a church in a town nearby, they commissioned us to replace the broken elements."

Looking almost like some kind of lantern with a fancy hat, the chimneys are crafted in three separate pieces: a closed tube sits atop the roof tiles, and a tube with open slats lets the smoke out. Topping it off is a conical "hat" with a cone-shaped pommel.

Left: *A pile of hand-thrown terra-cotta chimneys is for sale at the showroom of Fratelli Berti.*
Right: *A terra-cotta chimney tops a roof in Umbria.*

BRINGING IT HOME: Roofs

To re-create the look of a rustic Italian roof, nothing ranks above choosing the right tiles. You will want to combine rounded ones, called *coppe* in Italian (usually referred to as "caps" in English), with a flatter, more ridged, tile shape. The choices include Italian salvaged and handmade new tile, as well as options made in many other countries (see resources, page 224). Your general contractor can obtain detailed information from these companies concerning installation requirements.

Installing a roof is a serious investment. If your goals are less ambitious, consider adding an Italian-style chimney or two to your existing roof. These are often among the more whimsical aspects of an Italian farmhouse's profile. Using fire brick, you can copy some of the chimneys presented here or create your own designs.

Above: *A restored farmhouse roof has authentic touches such as salvaged antique tiles, copper gutters, and a brick chimney.* **Right:** *The crumbling forms of an old chimney in Umbria oozes with character.*

CHAPTER SIX

---
*

WINDOWS

---
*

I talian architecture can overwhelm us with its beauty, as when the setting sun glows against the travertine bulk of the Colosseum. But we are just as likely to be smitten with the more subtle details, such as the ray of light that angles in through a narrow stone-framed window, hitting the floor just so. While most of us can't hope to bring the Tuscan sun into our rooms, we can at least understand the art of the Italian farmhouse window.

When they are restoring homes in Italy, the first question most owners ask is, why are those windows so small? Usually the owners want to make the windows bigger. Before proceeding with such a plan, however, you should keep in mind the constraints under which the original builders of these farmhouses were working.

*Previous spread: Terra-cotta tiles are set against a glass window at Loggiato, in Tuscany. This system was often used in farms to allow pigeons access to their nests. In this restoration, glass is added. **Opposite and above:** A ground-floor entryway has an archway inspired by the farmhouse tradition, when wide openings allowed for passage of heavy equipment and animals. The steel-framed glazing, however, recalls more urban and industrial solutions.*

Their ground floors, almost always given over to sheltering animals, had no windows at all. The only natural light that entered the room came through the doorway when the wooden doors were open. On the upper floors, cutting a window into a stone wall required skilled labor, which meant cost. Add to this the price of glass, and you can begin to see why windows were kept to a minimum.

Another consideration was weather. Thick stone walls are incredibly good insulators against heat and cold. Any time a wall is breached—by a window or door—the environment is compromised. With their rough wooden frames and thin panes of glass, large windows would allow precious warmth to escape in the cold months and let in heat during Italy's notoriously torrid summers.

Even though the Italian Renaissance is based on symmetry and balance—and the stately villas and palaces of Florence and Tuscany reflect that—Italian rustic architecture seems ruled by anarchy. Window openings dot farmhouse façades with no discernible pattern. None of the windows are very large, and some are downright tiny. Some windows seem too close to others, while the ghosts of windows past have obviously been bricked over. Whether we are aware of it or not, this seemingly haphazard display is what gives most farmhouses their charm. When adding rustic Italian–style windows to your home, consider placement, variation in size, and details such as number of windows as well as frame construction materials. While windows are obviously meant to let the light in, in Italy shutters are also essential for keeping the light and heat out.

Framing the Light

Once the mason created an opening in the wall, the farmer or a local carpenter often made the window frame itself. The material was wood, ideally the hardest local wood available: chestnut, oak, or sometimes cypress. These woods resist humidity and do not expand and contract with changes in temperature.

In the United States, the most typical type of window is the sash, or

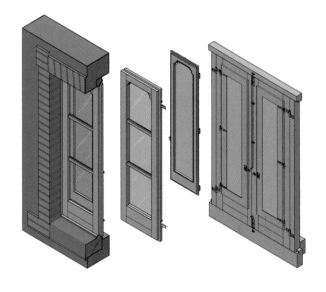

double-hung, window. In the rare cases where casement windows are used in the States and northern Europe, they usually open outward. In Italy, instead, the windows are casement windows, split vertically and always opening inward. In Italy the windows open inward because they are part of a complicated system that almost always includes outside shutters of some sort.

Although made of hardwood, the frame is still vulnerable to the elements. For this reason almost all rustic Italian window frames were painted. Typically pale gray, blue, or green oil-based paints were applied before the window was installed. Even though the layer of paint could protect the window frame for several years, it would need to be stripped down and reapplied, usually every few years.

A modern alternative is varnish. Transparent coats of this man-made (usually acrylic-based) material are not by any means traditional. Their upkeep, however, is much easier. A coat of varnish every three or four years, without stripping the frames down, should be enough to protect the wood, with occasional touch-ups in between.

*Opposite (from left to right): The finished window seen from the interior, with internal shutter, scuri, closed; one internal shutter, or scuri, ready to be attached; one side of the windowpane; a finished, and complete, window frame, mounted within the masonry surround of the wall. **Above:** The new blue/gray shutters were carefully copied from a set of antique shutters.*

Glass

Traditional farmhouse windows had handmade panes of glass usually measuring no more than I foot (30 cm) square. These were set into the larger frame and divided by cross frames. Remember that the expense of glass limited the size and number of the windows.

Today glass is less costly, but some homeowners still prefer the look of a multipane window. Ilaria Miani chose fixed-metal multipane frames—which are more common in industrial settings—for her home in Tuscany because she likes the modern look. "The final effect is something new and fresh, but speaks Italian," Miani says.

KEEPING THE LIGHT OUT

Shutters are a very environmentally friendly way of keeping a house cool. Non-Italians are often mystified when they are visiting a villa and the host comes along in the late morning to close all the shutters. Why not have a breeze blowing through the house on a hot day they wonder. Italians know better. By blocking the hot breeze from entering the house in midday, they can keep the house fresh and cool. The windows—and shutters—are then opened up after sunset, to allow the cooler evening air to refresh the house.

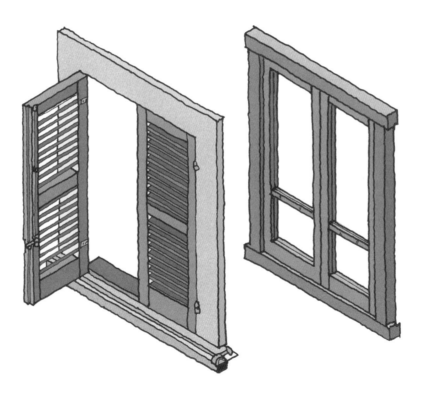

Opposite: A modern steel window frame is set deep into the existing walls of a home in Tuscany. The angled opening brings more light into the room while framing the picture-perfect view.
Above: Italian windows often comprise not only the frame, but also a set of shutters built into the external wall.

Outside Shutters

Almost all country houses in Italy have external shutters. At their most simple, the shutters are solid pieces of wood, which are hinged on the exterior wall to either side of the window. They swing shut and are closed, and locked, from the inside. They provide not only an extra layer of protection against the elements—shielding the fragile wood of the window frame—but added security as well. Farmhouses are almost always in isolated areas and are vulnerable to break-ins.

More sophisticated shutters provide options other than total closure. Slatted, louvered panels—*persiane*—allow air to come through, so that during the hot summer nights the shutters are closed but the inner windows remain open. Some shutters even have lower panels that hinge outward, to allow for more ventilation.

Inside Shutters

An additional system of interior shutters, located on the inner face of the window-panes, is called *scuri*. These thin shutters are usually hinged onto the wood frames surrounding the panes of glass. When the windows are closed, the *scuri* can be shut as well, to provide a darkness that is just about complete. In fact, *scuri* translates as "darkeners," and these shutters are usually closed at night, so that the morning light cannot make its way in.

Opposite: Of the dozens of small windows that originally dotted the façade to let air into this former tobacco-drying warehouse, two were left in place. Above: A shutter, called scuri, *is attached to the interior of this bedroom window in Todi, Umbria. At night it is closed against the glass, to keep the room perfectly dark for sleeping.*

Opposite: A wooden frame, varnished to protect it from the elements, is set into the stone wall of this home in Tuscany. The frame and sill are made from a local gray stone. **Top:** Ilaria Miani created a window seat in her home in Tuscany. **Above:** Both these meticulously reproduced door and window shutters were based on antique designs.

Left: Ilaria Miani chose to keep the window designs at Zingoni, her home in Tuscany, simple. The casement windows are painted a gray-blue and no external shutters were used. During the summer months, the blue cushion turns the low wall outside into a comfortable seat. ***Right:*** At a castle in Umbria, an unused doorway was sealed off with stonework, but the ghost of the original frame still shows through.

Left: Mixing old and new architectural elements can bring striking results. Here, a steel window in a minimalist stone frame provides contrast with the more rustic stone paving below. *Right:* A triangular pattern created with terra-cotta tile is set against glass windows, which bring light into a guesthouse. The design is based upon a traditional method of cross-ventilation used to dry hay.

A window is obviously not a freestanding object but part and parcel of the wall. The way the wall is constructed, and how it is opened to accommodate the window, is a key element in its design. Walls in Italian homes are usually about 2 feet (60 cm) thick, and the opening where the window is placed is correspondingly deep. The window is set into this deep niche flush with the exterior surface of the wall. To allow the maximum amount of light to enter the interior, the wall edges flanking the window are cut at an angle.

The solidity of Italian construction is especially evident in the window openings. Even if your walls are not constructed of 2 feet of stone, it is important to maintain this depth. In Oregon, where Domenico constructed an Italian rustic–style home, the drywall construction was designed to convey this sense of depth and massiveness.

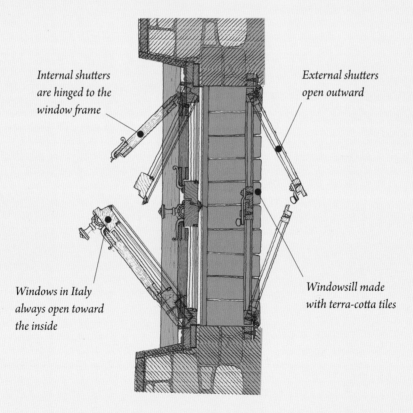

Internal shutters are hinged to the window frame

External shutters open outward

Windows in Italy always open toward the inside

Windowsill made with terra-cotta tiles

The Italians have developed intricate systems for setting windows and shutters into deep stone walls. The diagram shows how it's done.

In Italy, great efforts are made to adapt window designs to a particular setting in order to modulate the amount of light and air in a room. In this Todi home, the French door opens onto a small balcony. The floor-to-ceiling door is split horizontally, with a glass pane on the upper section. A small inner shutter, or scuri, is set against the glass, on the inside, to block sun when necessary.

WROUGHT IRON | GUALTIERO BRUNELLI

MARSCIANO, UMBRIA

While stones and tiles might survive for centuries and can be reused, everyday items such as railings and gratings—made out of wrought iron—usually have to be re-created from scratch. And this is when you need an artisan who truly knows the traditional methods of his craft. One of the best wrought-iron workers in Umbria is Gualtiero Brunelli, who learned the craft from his father. Today, at age eighty-two, he is passing this tradition on to his son-in-law Giuseppe. "Many ironsmiths become very proud of their artistic talent, and try to create very new and shiny, one-of-a-kind objects," says Domenico. Gualtiero understands that it can be even harder

Left: Gualtiero Brunelli at work in his laboratorio in Umbria. After heating a piece of wrought iron in the forge until it is red hot, he places it atop the anvil, where he will beat it into a fanciful curl (middle). Right: The finished product.

SCREENS

Whether Domenico is restoring an ancient home in Italy or building an Italian rustic home abroad, screens can be an issue. Twenty years ago in Italy, screens were almost unheard of. When Americans began buying homes in Italy, and importing the very reasonable request that they not be woken up in the night by mosquitoes, not much in the way of screen tradition existed. (With American-style sash windows, the problem is more easily solved.) Now, however, Italians have caught on, and a type of roll-down screen is available. This attaches to the upper frame of the window opening, between the glass and the outer shutter. You can easily pop the screen up to open and close the external shutters. But it is something that must be planned from the beginning, since space must be allocated for the mechanism.

In Domenico's design for Tenuta Santa Croce, a small inn in Umbria, traditional screens were set flush with the interior wall, while green shutters close from the outside. A roll-down screen was built into the window, just visible as the black strip at the top of the frame.

BRINGING IT HOME: WINDOWS

Windows are an integral part of the initial construction of any home. If you are lucky enough to be building from scratch, keep these things in mind when planning with your architect or designer:

- Stagger window placement and size, Italian-style.
- Make walls thick enough to add depth to window openings.
- Try to find a supplier or craftsman who can build wooden casement windows that open inward.

If you are working on an existing structure, consider installing just one essential aspect of the classic Italian window: exterior shutters. Even if they don't work, try to make the shutters look functional. Also ensure that each shutter measures half the width of the window, so that if you could actually close them, they would meet in the middle. For more information, see resources, page 225.

Above: *A deeply set window in a dining room in Umbria contains an antique stone sink, which acts as a sill.* **Opposite:** *A tiny window, set deep into the niche in the wall, was the original source of light for this room at Loggiato in Tuscany.*

CHAPTER SEVEN

DOORS

In our own restored farmhouse, there is one category of item that everyone notices right away: the doors. We spent the entire year prior to construction searching out the fourteen antique doors that now grace our home. While we were lucky enough to be able to shop for doors in Tuscany and Umbria, there are many other options available to capture this look. Domenico has learned over his years of both restoring and building homes that doors—interior and exterior—are among the most important design elements in a house. Even if you choose traditional-style doors, there is much room for creativity.

Previous spread: At Porte del Passato, in Umbria, salvaged wood was used to create new doors that look antique and incorporate handwrought hardware. **Opposite:** *This new portone, or main door, was crafted according to a traditional design.* **Above:** *A detail from a salvaged door, with its orginal wrought-iron fittings.*

EXTERIOR DOORS

Like many of the elements described in this book, doors have a strong architectural tradition in Italy. Historically, external doors came in two varieties. The entrance door was called the *portone*, or "large door." There was only one main entrance door, since the living area was located on the second floor and reached by a single staircase. This door was one of the strongest and largest in the house. There were other external doors, on the ground floor, called *mercantile*. Since the ground floor was the domain of animals and given over to farm use, the doors here were rougher in appearance.

Portone

Portone were important doors in all senses of the word. They had to be sturdy enough to protect the house from intruders. At the same time, they often acted as the most visible clues to a family's wealth. As a result, homeowners would spend as much money as possible on a door. The *portone* usually consisted of two sections, divided vertically down the middle. The left side remained fixed and was opened only to allow for the passage of large objects (furniture in, coffins out!). The right side was the working door, used by the family on a daily basis. Each section of the door consisted of a series of vertical planks, which faced the interior of the house. The outside face was divided into rectangular frames.

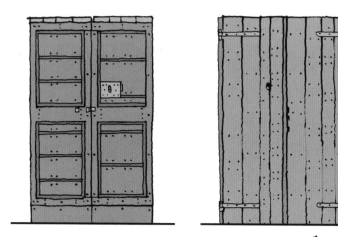

Above: The second-floor portone *usually consists of double doors that open inward. The exterior side (**left**) is often highly decorated and divided into panels. The interior (**right**) is flat and usually made of vertical planks. Both sides are put together with large iron nails.*

Mercantile

Mercantile, the heavy, more rustic doors used on the ground floor, were also made of two layers of wood. The inner layer was vertical slats, which were nailed to horizontal slats of varying widths on the front. The pieces were attached with iron nails, usually hand-forged, hammered in a haphazard pattern on the exterior.

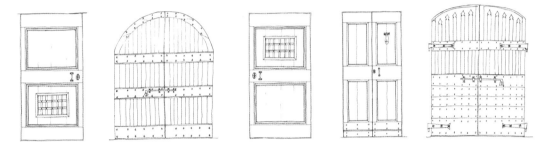

Above: Portone *and* mercantile *come in many different designs. Portone consists of one or two panels, often with a metal grille. Mercantile always consists of two parts, with a curved top set into an arched opening.* **Below:** *A new set of doors and shutters at Tenuta Santa Croce in Umbria. The original ground-floor opening would have had only a set of wooden doors. Today, arched French doors—in addition to exterior wooden* mercantile—*lets light into the large living room.*

INTERIOR DOORS

Inside the Italian farmhouse, doors were also handcrafted by artisans. Each usually consisted of a single panel of wood that had been finished in a decorative manner. The wood was often waxed to create some level of shine and protection. Some doors were painted, in some cases with scenes set into panels within the frames.

Antique doors are fairly easy to find. Salvaged from old farmhouses and buildings, these remnants of the past can be integrated into any setting. The problem is that no two doors are the same size, and so it is hard to plan until you have all your doors in hand. Fitting antique doors into a new setting requires skill and patience. The alternative is to commission new doors, made from old wood by artisans. Since the Italian artisans who make these doors are usually working with the same tools and materials as their ancestors, it is often hard to distinguish old from new. If the artisan is working with salvaged, aged wood, the result is even more authentic. "It's amazing how many people ask if these are the original doors to the house," says Laura Evans of the newly constructed chestnut doors that lead into her entrance hall in Umbria. A local carpenter crafted the doors out of antique wood, with wrought-iron fittings that were also made by hand.

Previous spread, left: In a formal palazzo in Todi, Umbria, polished oak doors are set into an entrance archway. A half-moon shaped grill above the portal allows natural light into the room even when the doors are closed. Overleaf: Formal Italian villas display elegant solutions. At Palazzo Terranova in Ronti, Umbria, a Palladian archway has a set of French doors leading out to the second-floor landing of a double-sided stone staircase.

Many styles of doors are still made by hand in Italy, including ones made from reclaimed wood (above) or hand-carved and painted by artisans (opposite).

BUILDING NOTES: HARDWARE

Italian doors have their own sets of hinges, locks, handles, and mechanisms for swinging shut and closing. Often hand-forged, usually in iron, the hardware can be one of the most interesting elements of a door. Round pull handles, intricate gratings, and ornate hinges are at once practical and decorative. Even the nails, which hold the two sides of the door together, can be applied so that the heads form a decorative pattern on the front of the door.

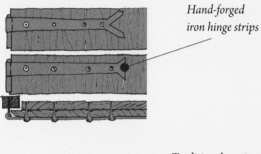

Hand-forged iron hinge strips

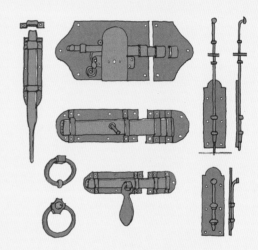

Traditional grating called "occhio abbotato"

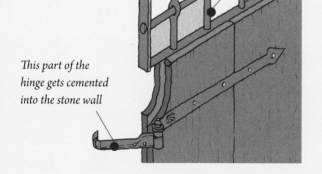

This part of the hinge gets cemented into the stone wall

Examples of handles, locks, and sliding closures found in old doors

Top left: An iron knob, mounted on the outside of a front door, is used to pull the door shut, but connects to no internal mechanism. *Top right:* The horizontal element in this wrought iron lock lifts upward, controlling the closure on the other side. *Above:* The interior of a portone usually has several wrought iron fixtures, including a ring to pull the door shut and a horizontal bar that locks it from the inside.

HAND-CRAFTED DOORS | PORTE DEL PASSATO

PISTRINO, PERUGIA

When we restored our Umbria home in Todi, we decided to incorporate antique doors in our design. But doing so wasn't easy: finding fourteen doors took a lot of time and effort. Then, each opening in the wall had to be made to fit each door. It was like a jigsaw puzzle consisting of door-size pieces. Fortunately, in recent years, skilled artisans have responded to the rising demand for antique doors and now craft new doors using aged wood, making the process much easier.

Porte del Passato is a family-run business in Umbria that specializes in providing doors for farmhouse restorations. When people started buying old homes to restore in Tuscany and Umbria in the last twenty or thirty years, they needed doors. Even if they could reuse some of the original doors, restoration work meant opening up new doorways, especially on the ground floor, which had originally been animal stalls. Enzo Belli started Porte del Passato twenty years ago to meet this need. The firm was already in the salvage business, and so began offering not only original antique doors salvaged from other buildings, but also newly made doors, crafted from old wood.

Left: At Porte del Passato, near Citerna, in the province of Perugia, antique salvaged beams are cut into planks. **Right:** The wood is then assembled into doors, which look antique and are difficult to distinguish from the real thing.

Although Porte del Passato has a collection of more then fifteen hundred antique doors for sale, its real business is the creation of reproduction doors. Using salvaged beams and flooring gathered from demolished houses throughout Italy, Belli and his team of carpenters craft doors using ancient techniques. "The end result is extraordinary," says Domenico. "It is almost impossible to tell the doors Belli makes from old ones."

The starting point is the wood itself. Chestnut, pine, and old poplar beams and flooring are cleaned up a bit, without removing their original patina. The doors are then crafted according to ancient designs. Once the doors are constructed, the wood is finished, or aged, using a process that is a carefully guarded secret. The door is then polished with *gomma lacca,* or seed lac, and natural beeswax.

While most farmhouses had simple, rustic wooden doors, Belli also reproduces a range of beautiful painted doors of the type more commonly found in villas and palaces. For these the wood is covered with a layer of gesso, then painted by a skilled artisan. Once the design is finished, the door is aged and then waxed.

Left: *New wood can be treated for an aged appearance, then used to create doors.*
Right: *Some doors are hand-decorated using natural pigments and gilding.*

BRINGING IT HOME: DOORS

A rustic Italian–style door can add so much texture to a home. Fortunately, doors can be easily retrofitted into a house. Salvaged doors—whether imported from Italy or scavenged from buildings in the United States—are available from suppliers of architectural artifacts (see resources, page 225). Antique doors are in the same category as furniture: expect them to cost what you would pay for any vintage piece. An alternative is to seek out new custom doors with an antique appearance. Many door makers specialize in new doors that look old.

Vintage doors come in all shapes and sizes, and a skilled craftsman can adapt them to fit almost any opening. Still, a much easier alternative is to commission new doors constructed from salvaged wood. This combines the patina of old wood with the ease of modern installation. Often the same suppliers that offer salvaged doors also make new doors from reclaimed wood.

*Above: Delicate hand-painted panels are set into this door, for sale at Porte del Passato. **Opposite:** This door, while antique, has been modified with the insertion of glass panels, which allow light to enter the room. Original farmhouse doors were always of sturdy wooden construction.*

CHAPTER EIGHT

FIREPLACES

I have a neighbor in Umbria, a farmer's wife, whose rough and practical approach to life on a working farm means that everything has a defined use. From dawn to dusk she takes care of everything and everyone—from husband to sheep, from roast chicken to vegetable garden. Yet even Marisa succumbs to the romance of the fireplace, her home's central focus. I was surprised to see the hearth lit even on a warm May day. *Ci fa compagnia*, "It keeps me company," she told me, shrugging her shoulders. The fireplace plays such an integral part of rural farmhouse life that it becomes almost like another member of the family. Though substantial, built of mortar, bricks, stone, and wood, this history-filled element can be added to almost any home.

*Previous spread: The fireplace that Domenico designed for the Twists in Umbria is crafted from stone, with the base raised off the floor about 20 inches (50 cm). **Opposite:** Ilaria Miani puts a modern spin on the traditional hearth in her restored farmhouse in Tuscany. **Above:** Small wood-burning cast-iron stoves were often the only source of heating in original farmhouses.*

THE NEW FAMILY HEARTH

Even when one is restoring a farmhouse in Italy, the hearth is almost always created from scratch. This is because the living room and the kitchen are usually relocated to the ground floor, where there is no original hearth. In Italian restorations, owners try to salvage materials from the original hearth to use in creating a new one. Paving stones, beams, stone corbels, and even carved mantelpieces from dismantled buildings are all used to create a new fireplace.

Materials

In traditional farmhouses, the fireplaces were often so big that families could almost sit inside them. In their home in Umbria, Kate Ganz and Daniel Belin were able to retain the massive proportions of a rustic hearth while tinkering with the design so that it became more functional. The 8-foot-long (2.5-m) mantelpiece, constructed from an antique chestnut beam, spans the entire width of the hearth. But rather than have the fire situated directly in the center of the opening, a separate and smaller fireplace was created within the opening. Raised on a stone base and separated from the rest of the niche by a wall of firebricks, the fire is able to burn

strongly, and the smoke is easily funneled up into the hood. The balance of space is used to store firewood.

The perfect fireplace in terms of draft is the result of a series of complicated formulas—but it also involves a bit of luck. Two elements that certainly affect the success of the draft are the size of the opening and the height of the chimney. The rule is to create as narrow an opening as possible, combined with a long and wide chimney. One of the challenges when using a salvaged mantelpiece is that if you calculated the optimal chimney height on the basis of the existing mouth, you would have to build a ridiculously high chimney to ensure good draft. An alternative is to narrow the opening with bricks or stones.

*Opposite: The fireplace in Kate Ganz and Daniel Belin's home in Umbria was assembled from salvaged items: an old oak beam, a pair of stone corbels, and reclaimed bricks. **Above:** Fireplaces allow for design creativity. The example on the left includes a plaster hood and is from a palace in Florence. On the right, simple slabs of stone form the mantelpiece.*

If you look at old Italian land records and maps, you will see a curious thing. Each small home is usually referred to by a notation marking the number of *fuochi*, or fires. Since each family had its own fireplace—and only one per family—this was a way of keeping the census. There was usually one main room per family, and each household had its own hearth on which to cook.

RUSTIC HEARTHS

Fireplaces in farmhouses were as big as space and budget allowed. They were located on the second floor, in the central room, which acted as both kitchen and living room. The entire family congregated there when they weren't sleeping, since it was the only room with heating.

The mantelpiece was usually 5 feet (150 cm) from the base, and the width could measure 6 feet (180 cm) or more. The mantel usually rested on a massive oak beam, which in turn sat on a pair of masonry walls, one to either side. Although some of these fireplaces were deep, the majority were relatively shallow, allowing much of the heat generated by the flames to be radiated out into the room.

Unfortunately, with heat comes smoke. Talk to almost anyone who grew up in the countryside, and you'll learn that their childhood memories inevitably include the sting of smoke in their eyes and the smell of fire in their clothes. As picturesque as these huge open fireplaces were, their proportions meant that they never drew very well.

UPSCALE ALTERNATIVES

Ornate villas or palaces had more fireplaces per home (at times one in every room), in different shapes and sizes. These fireplaces were made of precious materials such as marble and travertine, carved into patterns. Today, antique and salvage dealers often stock original mantelpieces that have been dismantled.

One of the nicest things to do on a cold winter day is to sit by the fire. At Loggiato, in Tuscany, guests can actually sit within the embrace of the fireplace, which has been designed with a sitting nook located beneath the large hood.

Cooking with Fire

An irresistible touch in a rustic Italian kitchen is a cooking hearth. To make a fireplace where you can cook, raise a regular fireplace about 18 inches (45 cm) from the ground. At this height, it will be comfortable to bend over and tend the coals.

Another option is to incorporate the fireplace into the countertop. This plan requires quite a bit of counter space and works best in a masonry kitchen. The countertop must be deep enough to enable you to pull out embers, yet still be covered by the hood. (Smoke from cooking can be intense.) The base must also be made of firebricks. A fire base slightly lower than the countertop also helps to contain the embers and ashes and is easier to clean.

A plan in the kitchen that requires less space is to locate the fireplace in the corner. The corner of a countertop is often hard-to-use space anyway, and since the corner is deep to begin with, it works well for cooking. Gonzola, one of more than a dozen restored farmhouses on the La Foce estate in Tuscany, has a hearth in the corner of its kitchen. The huge masonry hood hovers over the entire countertop, and not only draws the smoke of the fireplace but also acts as the hood for the cooktop.

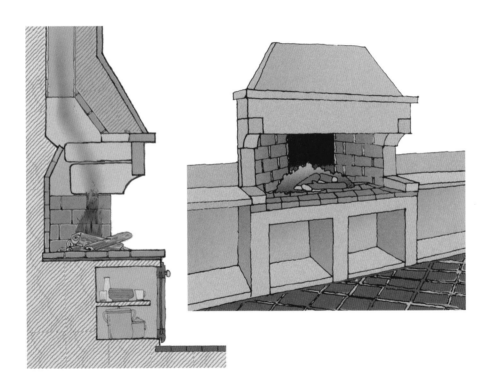

Opposite left: The corner of a kitchen countertop can often be a hard-to-use space. A corner fireplace requires less space, and its depth works well for cooking. This guesthouse kitchen in Umbria has a corner hearth with a small metal hood to draw smoke. *Opposite right:* In this Tuscan kitchen, a countertop fireplace is used for grilling while a traditional wood-burning stove, also called a cucina economica, is used for preparing food. *Above:* A wood-burning fireplace built into the kitchen makes it easy to grill all year long. The trick to making it useful—and safe—is to design it deeply enough so coals can be brought forward from the flames. The use of fire-resistant brick and stone is essential.

An antique carving was used to create the mantel of a new fireplace.

SALVAGE YARDS | LACOLE

Città di Castello, Umbria

Many Italian farmhouses, left to the elements for centuries, often are nothing more than four crumbling walls. To find authentic materials, Domenico's first stop is always a salvage yard. He has found full sets of steps, weathered terra-cotta roof tiles, and collections of glazed majolica tiles. One of Domenico's most reliable sources is Lacole, in Umbria. "Since they export, working with them is a way for me to inject a bit of authenticity into projects outside of Italy," he says.

Lacole was started by Dante Radicchi about fifty years ago. He began by stock-piling salvaged wooden beams from dismantled buildings in Umbria and Tuscany. He eventually traveled throughout Italy and amassed a collection that now includes roof tiles, flooring, fireplaces, sinks, and garden statues. His daughter, Velea, took over the business a few years ago and has expanded it to include a 320,000-square-foot (30,000 sq. m) warehouse.

Lacole carefully removes any damaged or cracked elements before batching items for shipping. Another plus is that they tamper with the antique materials as little as possible. "We try to leave the pieces exactly as we find them," Velea says. "Even if they have a little dirt on them, I would rather err on the side of doing too little. When you are buying old tiles, or a fireplace, I think you're partly paying for a bit of age and wear, no?"

Left: Lacole's ever-changing offerings include a vast array of salvaged fireplaces and mantelpieces.
Right: Architectural elements, like corbels and stone slabs, can be assembled to create new fireplace designs.

BRINGING IT HOME: FIREPLACES

For an antique fireplace, seek out dealers in architectural artifacts and antiques (see resources, page 226). Many offer mantelpieces imported from Italy, from hand-carved Baroque versions to quieter statements in dark gray *pietra serena* from Tuscany. Alternatively, you can design your own hearth. Try mixing reclaimed timbers with handmade or vintage brick, or any materials that have patina and soul.

If you already have a hearth, and just want to dress it up a bit, *all'italiana*, you can shop for handmade or antique wrought-iron accessories. Many companies export made-in-Italy fireplace implements, from andirons to pokers, tongs, and shovels.

Above: Look to local salvage yards to find stone architectural elements with an Italian feeling.
Opposite: Dan Blagg and Francesco Bianchini discovered this black marble mantelpiece at a local antique shop and installed it in their living room, adding a vintage Victorian electric fire to provide warmth.

CHAPTER NINE

STAIRCASES

Part of the charm of Italian farmhouses is that they often look more like small villages than single-family homes. Roofs vary in height and slope, and there is rarely a single, dominant façade. Among the most distinctive elements that animate buildings are an external staircase or two. While stone steps might be beautiful and quaint, with pots of geraniums and basil perched on each ledge, there is a real and practical reason behind their construction. In this chapter we will look at staircases from both a structural and a decorative point of view. We will also explore the materials used to create these steps, discovering ways to work them into new settings. The materials used to create rustic staircases, as well as their placement and design, can all be easily adopted and adapted for any building.

Previous spread: The owners added the grand double staircase at Palazzo Terranova when they restored the villa in Ronti, just north of Perugia, to create a small boutique hotel. The classic forms of the balustrade, and the Palladian arch beneath it, were handcrafted from pietra serena *by local artisans.* **Opposite:** *Terra-cotta tiles are used in rustic Italian stair construction.* **Above:** *In more formal settings, such as the garden at La Foce, large slabs of stone provide an elegant solution.*

INSIDE OR OUTSIDE

The External Stairs

When we build a home today, it is almost always for a single family. But Italian farmhouses were multifamily affairs: each family (think two brothers, plus wives and children) had their own separate, complete apartment on an upper floor. The ground floor housed the most important tenants on the farm: cows, chickens, rabbits, and pigs.

While this may sound like tight quarters, the two areas experienced a very strict separation. Large doors on the ground floor opened directly onto the farmyard, and the upper floors were reached via an external staircase that ran up the side of the house. There was no internal connection between the animals' ground floor and the families' upper floors. This segregation ensured that the inevitable concomitants of raising animals—noise, smells, dirt, and bugs—would stay with the animals.

When city people restore Italian farmhouses as second homes, the first thing they do is transform the ground floor into the main living area. Not so for farmers who remain on their land. Even if the family no longer has cows and horses, the ground floor is still kept separate from the living quarters and used for storage of farm equipment, supplies, and food.

Obviously, for modern life an external staircase can't be the only way to get from one floor to another. Although we may like the *style* of Italian rustic living, we don't necessarily want to import chickens and cows into what will be the living room and kitchen. We would also like to be able to come downstairs without getting out an umbrella. That said, we can certainly apply some of the materials and building techniques used in external staircases to inside steps.

This staircase is one of several at Chiarentana, in Tuscany. Each one leads from the courtyard to second-floor apartments, since the ground floor would have originally been dedicated to farm use.

BUILDING NOTES: BUILDING A STAIRCASE

External staircases are constructed using the same materials and techniques as for external walls—stone or masonry, sometimes covered in plaster. A foundation is laid down, and then stone is used to form the support for the steps. Historically, the large space created beneath the slope of the stairs was always put to use, for storage or as a location for an outdoor oven to bake bread.

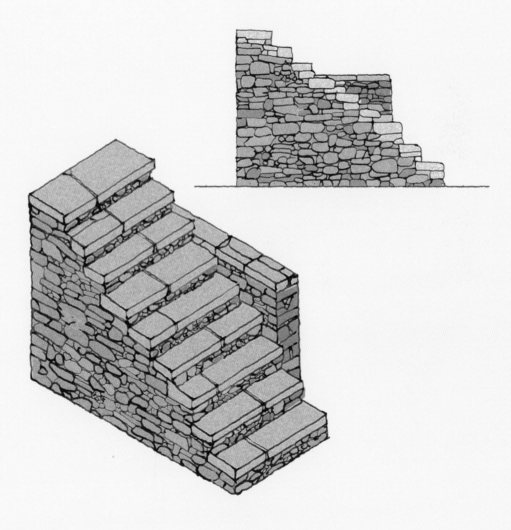

External staircases were often constructed of stone, in the same manner as stone walls. The treads were either of terracotta, or—as shown here—large slabs of stone, a more costly solution.

The Inside Stairs

Inside the house, the issue is space. An interior staircase can take up an enormous amount of precious room. Aesthetics are also a concern; you may not want a large block of masonry inside your home. Several alternative—but traditional—methods of construction can be used. One is to support the staircase with a vaulted structure. A load-bearing archway holds the weight of the stairway, leaving the space beneath free.

An alternative is to use wooden beams to hold the weight, with smaller beams and tiles forming the actual stairs. This method is the same as that used in building a roof, but the slant is greater. We chose this method when adding an internal staircase in our own home in Umbria. It freed up the space beneath the staircase, thus making the smallish dining room–entry hall seem bigger. An added bonus was the almost sculptural impact of the supporting beams.

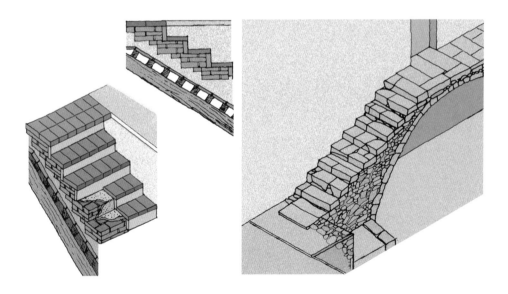

*In Italy, one of the most common methods of creating a staircase (**above left and center**) is to use wooden beams as supports. Large beams are set at an angle, holding smaller cross beams that in turn support terra-cotta tiles. A layer of concrete then supports the stairs themselves, which are usually constructed of brick. The finishing layer consists of either terra-cotta tile or large slabs of stone. **Above right:** In this more unusual method, a supporting arch supports the staircase. **Opposite:** A stone wall acts as a support for a newly built staircase. Space beneath the stairs was put to use as a coat closet.*

Two Staircases Are Better Than One

Although it might seem crazy to build an external staircase as your only means of getting from one floor to another, creating one *in addition* to an internal staircase is a great idea. The Twists in Orvieto chose to keep the outdoor staircase, even though they also created one inside. The steps that originally led to the second-floor kitchen now lead to a small terrace that opens off the master bedroom. "It's a wonderful solution," Carolyn says. "The terrace that it creates is extremely private but at the same time has direct access to the garden. And we find ourselves often sitting on the steps themselves, which have become a gathering point."

Similarly, Domenico recently designed a new home in Santiago, Chile, with two staircases. Although the external staircase, which leads to the second-floor living room, certainly wasn't necessary (there is, of course, an internal one, leading from the entrance hall), it added a sense of surprise and movement that makes the building feel like an Italian farmhouse. "It is always tempting to streamline things when designing a new house," explains Domenico. "But I find that adding things that don't necessarily have a use—like an external staircase—can give a new house a quirky, old feeling."

Opposite: *The Twists in Umbria chose to retain the original exterior staircase in their restored farmhouse. Although there is also a staircase inside, the exterior one is still used to gain access to the private terrace (**above**) located off the master bedroom.*

MATERIALS: FROM STEPS TO RAILS

One of the easiest things we can borrow from tradition when building a staircase is choice of materials. Since simplicity is the key, it is wise to use the same materials you chose for the floor. For instance, if you have terra-cotta tiles for floors, then terra-cotta would be a good choice for the treads of the stairs. The risers can be of a similar material but are more often plastered masonry, which is then painted. It is more fragile than terra-cotta and must be repainted periodically, but it gives a lighter and less modern look.

The Tiled Stair

The terra-cotta tiles used on stairs may look the same as floor tiles, but they are actually quite different. Since treads stick out over the edges of the steps by about 1 inch (2.5 cm), these tiles have to be thicker to prevent cracking under the weight of people stepping on them. They are usually about double the thickness of floor tiles. They can be ordered with a beveled edge, usually rounded, to create an elegant look. A more rustic effect is a simple straight edge.

Left and right: When choosing materials, it is always best to keep things simple. Since the flooring is handmade terra-cotta, the stairs are also paved in the same material.

The Grand Stair

In palaces and villas, interior flights of stairs were often made of stone or marble, and certain of these more formal decorative elements can be borrowed for today's rustic architecture. Salvage yards in Italy are great sources of entire flights of stone or marble steps from preexisting buildings. These flights are sold either as separate treads or as wedge-shaped elements that form both tread and riser. The steps— made out of local stones like *pietra serena* or travertine—can add a well-worn and beautiful feeling to a home.

At Palazzo Terranova in Umbria, carved stone steps fit perfectly with the formal interior.

Railings

When staircases are outside the house, the hand railings are usually formed by extension of the external supporting wall. At Palazzolaccio, Ilaria Miani's home in Tuscany, the original external staircase was restored, and the stone wall supporting the stairs extends about 3½ feet (107 cm) above the stair base to form a sloping wall along the outer edge of the steps. The upper edge of the wall is finished with 2-inch-thick (5-cm) slabs of pale gray *pietra serena*, the stone that also forms the treads.

*Left: A hand-painted stairwell adds life to an entry hall in Todi. **Right:** A handcrafted wrought-iron railing is an easy way to import a bit of rustic charm into any setting. **Opposite:** The external stone staircase at Casellacce, in Tuscany, a new addition, makes use of local materials like stone, brick, and carved* pietra serena *steps.*

TRAVERTINE | VASELLI MARMI

RAPALANO, TUSCANY

Even though travertine stone had no place in rustic farmhouses in central Italy, most people are tempted to use this honey-colored material—at least in some way—when restoring their homes. In fact, using local materials in new ways is one of the hallmarks of these farmhouse restorations, and one of the innovations that we can apply when emulating the rustic style in new homes or additions. "I love working with materials that have a history in this area," says Benedikt Bolza, architect of more than twelve houses at his family's estate, Castello di Reschio. "This allows me to use local materials, even when there is no tradition of an object to follow. For instance, there were no bathrooms in these buildings, so when you place a bathtub within this setting you have to be creative and give old materials new uses. I would never think of using a plastic tub, so I turn to stones such as *pietra serena* or local travertine for inspiration."

Left: At a travertine quarry in Rapalano, Tuscany, the famous honey-colored stone is reflected in the water. *Right:* Massive blocks of travertine are carefully cut from the walls of the quarry.

His favorite source is Vaselli Marmi, in Tuscany, not far from Siena. The family-run business specializes in a local stone, called *travertino di Rapolano*, a honey-colored travertine, as well as travertine from Tivoli, south of Rome, and several other stones from around the world. The travertine from Rapolano is both beautiful and strong, making it an ideal construction material. Danilo Vaselli, who owns the firm with his siblings, oversees the massive blocks of stone as they are cut from huge pits in the local quarry. Vaselli says the tradition of quarrying travertine goes back to the Etruscans. The stone was especially popular in the mid-nineteenth century, when many of the quarrying and carving methods were modernized. During the rebuilding boom in Italy following World War II, travertine was used to reconstruct bridges, roads, and buildings.

Today Vaselli Marmi specializes in architectural work. It can manufacture to almost any specifications, producing elements such as bathtubs and spiral stairs.

Left: *Even though Vaselli marble uses computer-driven machines to carve complicated shapes designed by architects and designer, the finishing touches, are still executed by skilled artisans.*
Right: *A set of travertine steps, at Vaselli, wait to be installed at the nearby Estate of Castello di Reschio, in Umbria.*

CHAPTER TEN

KITCHENS

The concept of a kitchen as a dedicated room is relatively recent in rural Italy. Formerly the chores—and joys—of daily life happened in the one main room of an Italian farmhouse. Cooking, eating, even sleeping took place not far from the hearth in the large, centrally located room. This is no longer the case. When we create a new kitchen in an Italian rustic–style home, we can draw on traditional elements while assembling a room that better fits modern life. For inspiration on finding new solutions within the rustic tradition, we can turn to farmhouse restorations in Italy, and apply the plans, materials, and craftsmanship that bring these rooms into the twenty-first century.

Previous spread: Laura Evan's kitchen in Umbria is completely new, but embraces the eclectic feeling of Italian rustic kitchens. Handmade artisanal elements are everywhere, from the terra-cotta and majolica tiles to the wooden beams that support the ceiling. **Opposite:** *Dan Blagg and Francesco Bianchini's warm and inviting kitchen in Todi centers on an antique wooden table.* **Above:** *Even practical elements are used for decoration, such as the copper pots that hang on the wall.*

REINVENTING THE ITALIAN KITCHEN

In traditional Italian farmhouses, the family's living area—including the kitchen—was located on the second floor, with shelter for animals below. So even when restoring a farmhouse in Italy, the kitchen is usually created from scratch since few people want this room up a flight of stairs. If building a new kitchen on the ground floor means that there is no picturesque, original hearth to work around, it also allows much more freedom to create something exciting and new.

One of the main stylistic characteristics of traditional Italian country kitchens was their eclectic yet practical nature. Nothing matched, things were added as they were needed, and everything had a use. If we keep this mantra in mind, the end result in our modern kitchens can be similar in spirit to traditional rooms.

One way to achieve this look is to bring together elements that don't match or look too obviously utilitarian. Instead of commissioning a built-in storage cabinet, the Twists in Orvieto chose an antique, glass-fronted cupboard to store dishes and glassware. Two separate freestanding sideboards flank the oven, and all the appliances—including the refrigerator and oven—are freestanding. Even though the ensemble of elements includes new appliances, the decor looks as if it came together over time, in keeping with the original spirit of Italian kitchens.

Dan Blagg and Francesco Bianchini chose a similar solution for their kitchen in Todi, mixing salvaged pieces with antiques. An antique sink—made of pink variegated marble—was rescued from Francesco's grandmother's cellar and installed next to a custom-built cabinet. Although the cabinet looks old, it was designed to accommodate a dishwasher below and their collection of china above. Dan and Francesco even managed to install a *cucina economica*, a wood-burning oven, within the preexisting fireplace, and a more practical electric oven as well.

Another way to embrace the eclectic is to mix old and new in bold ways. Italy is home to some of the most stunning appliance and fixture firms in the world. Sinks, taps, ovens, and cooktops are produced by cutting-edge design firms. "I love to mix sleek stainless-steel faucets with traditional materials," says Ilaria Miani, whose kitchens combine rustic elements such as rough wooden shelving with streamlined faucets and sinks. "From a design perspective, I think both styles—the modern and traditional—gain more impact when they rub up against each other," she says. In her home in Tuscany, Miani flanked the open hearth with a pair of extra-wide Zanussi ovens. The stoves are topped by a massive hood, supported by a hand-hewn chestnut beam.

*Opposite left: A butler's sink is set into a specially commissioned terra-cotta countertop. **Opposite right:** Mismatched, handmade majolica tiles form the kitchen backsplash at Loggiata, in Tuscany. **Below:** In the Twists' kitchen in Umbria, free-standing elements come together, mixing new appliances with handmade pieces.*

BACK TO THE HEARTH

A modern kitchen needs ovens and cooktops, *certo*. But why not also import the most seductive and heartwarming element in the tradition of *la cucina*, the hearth?

Today a fireplace can provide not only warmth but also a place to roast and grill. But the original design needs some tweaking. Traditional farmhouse fireplaces were large and open, with the fire at floor level. While this design allowed the most heat to enter the room, it also meant backbreaking work for anyone tending the grill. A modern alternative is to raise the fire base. This not only makes cooking easier but has an added benefit: the dancing flames and glowing coals become visible from the central table.

Above: *Two stainless-steel ovens flank a countertop open grill in this Tuscan kitchen restoration.*
Opposite: *The centerpiece of Kate Ganz and Daniel Belin's kitchen in Umbria is the rustic hearth. The large stone mantelpiece protrudes out into the room, hanging over the fire below. In a traditional farmhouse the hearth would have been lower, allowing more warmth—and smoke—into the room. Here the level has been raised, creating a smaller opening that improves the hearth's draft. The end result reduces smoke and makes grilling less backbreaking.*

The most important element in the main room of an Italian home, the fireplace was usually a huge affair, with a large open mouth, mantelpiece, and hood. The hood, made of plastered bricks, would rest on a long wooden beam or piece of stone, supported by two consoles on each side. In some areas of Italy, the fireplace was so large that benches were located under the hood for families to congregate in its warmth on winter nights.

More than just a heat source, the fireplace was also where the daily meals were cooked. This meant that the hearth was almost constantly lit. Even during the summer, the fire would be going—albeit at a lower level—to cook. Copper pots were hung by their handles on a system of chains and lowered or raised to increase or decrease the amount of heat. Meats were grilled directly over the coals, using a flat grill or a rotisserie. The rotisseries either were hand-cranked or had windup systems. Today they are still much used, although usually powered by electricity.

Even in Italian farmhouses with no plumbing, most central rooms had some sort of sink. This shallow basin—4 or 5 inches (10–12 cm) deep—was usually carved out of local stone, with a draining board located to one side. The sink drain was connected to a pipe that siphoned the water through a hole in the wall. Since indoor plumbing rarely existed, water was carried in from a well and poured from a pitcher as needed.

Above: Salvaged beams, antique bricks and reclaimed stones combine in a newly built fireplace that looks like an antique. Below: A salvaged pink marble sink is backed by a set of nineteenth-century Neapolitan tiles in this home in Todi.

Freestanding Elements

Besides the obligatory hearth and sink, the rest of the furnishings in an Italian farmhouse kitchen were a collection of mismatched elements that served specific purposes, usually in the preparation or consumption of food. Before the days of central islands and counters, there was the kitchen table. This was not only where the family gathered to eat meals; it also served as the only work surface in the room, the de facto countertop. Always made of wood, the table was as big as the room would allow, and surrounded by chairs.

Another essential piece of furniture was the *madia,* or flour storage cupboard. This multipurpose piece was usually constructed in two parts. The upper section, about chest to waist height, was hinged on top, much like a chest. The space inside was used once a week to let the dough rise for bread. Once the bread was baked, it was stored in this space. The hinged cabinet below was used to store flour. The entire piece was made very carefully, with tightly sealed closures, to ensure that field mice were kept away from both raw flour and finished bread.

An important addition to the country kitchen at the turn of the last century was the *cucina economica.* Essentially a wood-burning stove made of cast iron, it was "economical" since it used a lot less wood than a traditional fireplace. Although it never took the place of the fireplace, it allowed families to cook with no smoke, since the flue connected via a pipe to the outside. Rounding out the room was often a plate rack, usually over the sink, where dishes could dry and be easily stored.

Above: *A* cucina economica, *or wood-fueled, cast-iron oven, was a nineteenth-century innovation in Italy. It may look outdated, but it is still a wonderful way not only to cook, but also to heat a cold kitchen during winter.* **Overleaf:** *A kitchen in Umbria, designed from scratch, keeps many defining elements of a traditional rustic kitchen, including a massive oak table and freestanding cabinetry.*

Above: The kitchen at Casaccia, in Tuscany, mixed traditional elements with modern notes such as a stainless-steel hood. **Opposite:** This Umbrian kitchen features hand-painted, antiqued cabinet doors and hand-painted majolica tiles from nearby Deruta.

BUILDING NOTES: THE BUILT-IN OPTION

For a sleeker look, consider custom-made built-in cabinetry. In our own house in Umbria, we chose a traditional style, with carved cabinet doors that wrapped around one side of the room. The double set of ovens was set into this scheme, with the dishwasher hidden behind a cabinet door. We built a freestanding wooden *armadio* to contain and hide the refrigerator. The Twists, in Orvieto, chose a similar approach, with cabinetry that incorporates the sink.

Both of these kitchens were constructed by building a masonry framework first, then attaching handmade wooden doors. A more modern, and space-saving, option is to construct the entire kitchen of wood and have it set into place.

Decorative Touches: Walls and Floors

One of the most charming aspects of traditional Italian rustic kitchens is the fact that they didn't really *feel* like kitchens. The table and chairs, gathered around the open hearth, made them feel more like living rooms. With this in mind, the choices for wall and floor treatments become both easy and limitless.

Think of this room as you would any other space in your home. If you used terra-cotta tile for the floor in your dining room, you can use it here, too. Wide wooden planks, or even tinted cement, could work as well. The idea is that it should not feel kitcheny in a traditional sense but rather should flow with the rest of the house. And while you may want to protect the wall area above the sink and cook-top with tile or some other easily washable surface, the rest of the walls can be approached like the others in your home.

Since countertops and backsplashes have no real history in the Italian rustic kitchen, we are very free to be inventive with them. Add to this the fact that the surface to be covered is limited in size, and you realize that this is where one can sometimes indulge in more expensive choices, like salvaged antique tiles or hand-painted majolica. For instance, Kate Ganz and Daniel Belin found a set of matching nineteenth-century majolica tiles that provided a burst of color in their kitchen in Umbria. Ilaria Miani chose a local material—gray *pietra serena*—for her galleylike kitchen in Zingoni, in Tuscany. The Twists carried over the use of terra-cotta from the floor to the countertop and commissioned a set of oversize tiles—measuring 12 inches (30 cm) square—to form the counter at either side of the sink.

Opposite: Above left: Kate Ganz bought this set of salvaged blue-and-white tiles before she even knew where she was going to use them. They now work wonderfully as a backsplash in her kitchen in Umbria. Above right: In this Tuscan kitchen, restoration designer Ilaria Miani inserted an untraditional finish—unfinished concrete walls—to provide a minimal and modern feel. Below: Large slabs of terra-cotta were custom-ordered and act as the countertop in this Umbrian kitchen.

BRINGING IT HOME: Kitchens

The dominating theme in most Italian country kitchens is their eclectic decor. This allows a great deal of freedom for anyone trying to get this look. For storage pieces, one can search out antiques, or even new furniture, that were not necessarily designed for kitchen use. Almost anything goes, though to instantly get the look, try a heavy wooden table—a central feature of kitchens in most rustic Italian homes.

To add an Italian touch to an existing kitchen, try creating a backsplash of brightly colored, handmade tiles. Handmade tiles from Italy are widely available (see resources, page 227). If those are too pricey, seek out less expensive options from such places as Central and South America as well as China—many are quite attractive.

Another approach is to embrace traditional Italian materials, using them in a fresh, modern, and elegant way. Terra-cotta tiles, stone countertops, and Italian brand appliances make perfect partners.

*Above: Open shelving holds and displays a china collection. **Opposite:** A kitchen combines traditional rustic materials such as terra-cotta and local stone with newer ones, such as stainless-steel appliances.*

CHAPTER ELEVEN

BATHROOMS

W hen Domenico designs a bathroom in a rustic Italian farmhouse restoration, he likes to get creative. This is because
there are no firm rules. The history of indoor plumbing in the Italian
countryside is a short one, and as farmers incorporated running water
into their lives, the bathroom was given short shrift. Italian-style
bathrooms today represent a chance to create something completely
new while still incorporating materials, proportions, and textures
from Italian tradition.

*Previous spread: Traditional, local materials like aged chestnut and hand-carved travertine are
used in modern ways in this Umbrian bathroom.* **Opposite:** *A freestanding claw-foot tub sits atop
a unique flooring made up of black and white river stones set into cement in this luxurious bath
designed by Architect Benedikt Bolza.*

When indoor plumbing finally made its way into rural homes in Italy—generally in the late 1940s—people had to think about how to set aside space for personal hygiene. One common response was to tack a small room on to the upper floor. Often made out of bricks, these cubicles frequently protrude from stone houses like little Lego additions. They have a small window for ventilation and their own little tiled roofs. These rooms are almost painfully small and usually include a toilet, a small sink, and a half-size tub that is peculiar to Italy, with a small step-shelf, which you sit on while washing yourself with a handheld spray hose. Since water was likely to spray everywhere, the entire bathroom was usually covered in glazed tiles.

THE MODERN BATHROOM

Today Italy boasts some of the top bathroom fixture companies in the world. Choices for pieces used to furnish the bath—sinks, tubs, showers, taps—are almost overwhelming. Here are two approaches to consider.

Take Over a Room

If farmers tried to fit the bathroom into the smallest space possible, many new owners take the opposite approach. Rather than cordon off part of an existing room to function as a bath, one can take over an entire room and turn it into something truly extravagant. It may have little to do with tradition, but the results are often stunning.

"One of the things I find exciting is working within an existing structure. The restraints often lead me to new and unique solutions that in the end can be applied almost anywhere," says architect Benedikt Bolza. He tends toward the luxurious on his family's estate, Castello di Reschio, in Umbria, and places a sumptuous bathroom en suite with every bedroom in the homes he restores, designing extravagant tubs in each room.

At Palazzo Terranova in Umbria, a huge corner room measuring 15 by 18 feet (4.5 x 5.5 m) was converted into a magnificent bathroom. The focal point is a massive polished travertine tub, which sits in the middle of the room like sculpture. The tub was commissioned from stonemasons in Rapolano Terme, who took several months to carve it. Special steel beams were installed beneath the floor to support the extraordinary weight.

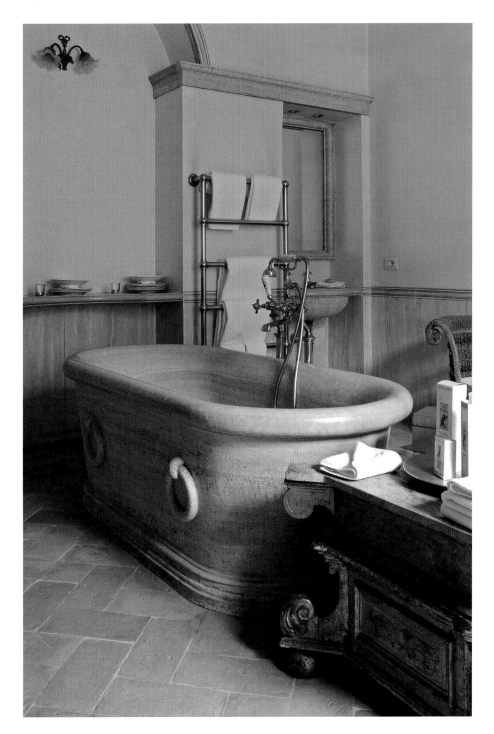

A local artisan sculpted the massive tub at Palazzo Terranova out of a solid block of travertine. The same stone was also used to craft the set of double sinks, as well as the vanity shelf.

Something New

Many homeowners prefer a contemporary bathroom look. Ilaria Miani has restored more than ten farmhouses in Tuscany and has very distinct opinions about bathrooms. "I hate that fake rustic look and try to avoid it throughout the houses. But I find it really has no place in the bathrooms, which are always completely new anyway!" she says. She makes a modern bath work in a traditional-style home by using materials that are local and traditional. One of her favorites is *pietra serena*, a dark gray stone that comes from nearby quarries and forms the sink and tub surrounds at Palazzolaccio.

Opposite: *Laura Evan's master bath opens onto a private terrace where an outdoor shower takes in the view of the Umbrian valley.* **Above:** *Ilaria Miani uses traditional elements in new ways. Travertine is sculpted into trapezoidal sinks, and dark* pietra serena *serves as the counter.*

Bolza uses traditional materials in new ways. When he chooses terra-cotta tiles, he inserts them within travertine to create new patterns and textures. *Pietra serena* creates a sculpturelike tub, almost Japanese in proportions. In one bathroom, the exposed stone walls bump up against the slick gray of a polished *pietra serena* shower stall. "What I love is the contrast: of old and new, or rough and smooth, that using traditional materials in new ways can provide," he says.

When planning where to place bathrooms, Miani is equally inventive. In the large master suite at Casellacce, she deconstructed the bathroom. The shower is tucked into a small space at one corner of the room, and the toilet on the other. Both have doors, which can be left open so that the windows from these small rooms let light flow into the main bedroom space. In between, two built-in closets flank a cozy window seat. This arrangement allowed her to keep the original proportions of the room, including the windows.

*Above: A series of small spaces is used to create a deconstructed bath at Ilaria Miani's home, Casellacce. **Opposite:** Salvaged majolica tiles, from Vietri in southern Italy, create a vivid pattern above a marble sink at Tenuta di Santa Croce in Umbria.*

BATHROOM TILE

A funny thing happened on the way to creating the modern Italian bathroom. At a certain point, Italians went tile crazy. Once bathrooms began to be incorporated into homes, owners and contractors decided that the entire room had to be tiled: from the floor to the ceiling, shiny, hard tiles protected every surface. While Italian architects and designers have begun to cut back on tile, most Italian contractors would like to cover every surface in glazed ceramics.

Even if you don't want floor-to-ceiling tiles, their allure is unmistakable. There are gorgeous tiles and mosaics that can be used—but they don't have to cover every single surface. Kate Ganz and Daniel Belin chose brightly colored, hand-painted antique tiles as a leitmotif in many of the baths in their home in Umbria. Since the number of tiles was limited, the architect designed an oak base that would make the most of the few they had.

At Loggiato, a small hotel in Tuscany, the owners, Barbara and Sabrina Marini, used majolica tile made by a friend. "The hexagonal shapes were meant to be installed vertically, but we decided to lay them out horizontally, mixing up the different patterns," Barbara explains. The tiles form the backsplashes in one of the guest bathrooms, above the sink and the tub.

Even though Laura Evans had only a handful of early-twentieth-century tiles from Naples, she was able to install a row of them to form a colorful backsplash to a sink in the guest bath. "The marble sink is actually from Asia, a modern import, but its aged look ended up working well with the chipped and nicked tiles," says Evans.

Using handcrafted tiles doesn't always mean a burst of rustic color. At Casaccia, in Tuscany, the handmade terra-cotta tiles are painted with a white glaze. Much different from industrial white tiles, these 6-inch (15-cm) squares are uneven, and the glaze forms a mixed palette of whites that creates an interesting surface.

Left: *A set of salvaged nineteenth-century tiles are set into a wooden base.* **Right:** *Hand-painted hexagonal majolica tile is set horizontally in this bathroom at La Loggiato in Tuscany.*

Left: Laura Evans used hand-painted tiles from Southern Italy to provide a colorful backsplash over a marble sink. *Right:* Handmade and hand-painted white tiles provide a rich, yet light finish in a bathroom in Casaccia, on the La Foce estate in Tuscany.

BRINGING IT HOME: BATHROOMS

Creating an Italian bathroom is not so much about a way of building as it is about choosing the right materials. You can't go wrong with authentic Italian stone such as *pietra serena*, travertine, and marble. Stone importers can help you to choose the perfect slab and will also craft it into any shape, from freestanding bathtubs to sink vanities. For another true Italian touch, remember that Italy is home to some of the most stylish bathroom fixture companies in the world, and most lines, like Cesame, are widely imported into the United States (see resources, page 227).

But you don't have to limit your choice to Italian elements. Salvage companies are a great source for vintage tubs, fixtures, and sinks. Even if they are not Italian, their old-fashioned styling will blend well in a Tuscan-inspired bathroom. For a lovely artisanal touch, hand-painted majolica tile—antique or new—can be used on almost any surface, from vanity tops to walls. These are widely imported from Italy, as well as from other places where they are made by hand, including Mexico and Asia.

Above: *Salvaged terra-cotta tiles are used to create a sink surround.* **Opposite:** *At Castello di Reschio, architect Benedikt Bolza chose Travertino Noce, a darker variant on travertine for the bathroom's floor and a wall.*

CHAPTER TWELVE

STORAGE

Storage in Italian homes is as much a cultural decision as an aesthetic or structural one. Traditional solutions are not—by today's standards—always the most convenient. But some classic storage designs are worth consideration; they are not only ingenious but good-looking as well.

Rustic Italian farmhouses were part working farm and part home. While storage was ample for essential items, such as hoes, tractors, and other farm implements, when you headed upstairs, where the families lived, storage became scarce. One of the reasons is simply that people had few things to store beyond a few sets of clothes, plates, pots, and bed linens. The concept of a built-in closet was not only unheard of but just not necessary.

Previous spread: Open shelving creates a divider between the kitchen and dining room at Casellacce and provides easy access to dinnerware from both rooms. **Opposite and above:** *Existing niches in the walls at Loggiato were put to good use. Simple wooden glass-fronted doors were installed and now display brightly colored ceramics.*

An antique plate rack was usually the only storage for dishware in rustic farmhouses. The open-bottomed shelves held the few dishes the family owned, doing double duty as storage and drying rack over the sink.

Instead, families had separate pieces of furniture used to store belongings. Large wooden chests were placed at the ends of the beds and held bed linens and blankets. These pieces of furniture usually arrived with the wife and contained her dowry (embroidered sheets, linens, et cetera). Each family generally had at least one standing *armadio,* or armoire, to hold clothes. And the kitchen had a plate rack to store dishes.

FREESTANDING STORAGE

The *Armadio*

The quintessential Italian piece of furniture must be the *armadio,* or armoire. These massive, two-doored items were the centerpieces of any Italian home. An *armadio* usually had a hanging rod in the main area, which was topped by a shelf. One or two drawers beneath offered extra storage. While they may not provide enough space to hang your entire wardrobe, you might consider one for a guest room, or even an entrance hall, to provide an instant feeling of old-world Italian living.

Kate Ganz painting this old armadio *bright red. Located in a guest room, it is spacious enough for a vacation's worth of clothes.*

Antique *armadi* can also be put to new uses. One of the first pieces of furniture we bought for our own home in Umbria was a massive, seventeenth-century oak *armadio*. We envisioned it as forming an essential part of our master bedroom. Reality set in when we realized that there was almost no space in our room where it would fit! Today its warm, worn form is in the guest suite and not only provides room for clothes and linen but hides the television, phone, and computer as well.

The *Cassapanca*

One of the easiest pieces of furniture to find at Italian antiques stores or fairs is a wooden chest, or *cassapanca*. These deep, heavy pieces open from the top and usually can be closed with keys. In farmhouses they were essential items, since precious bed linens could be stored in them and protected from mice and insects. They are still handy items for storing extra blankets or pillows. Carolyn and James Twist keep one at the end of the bed in their guest room, using it to store extra sheets. Kate Ganz and Daniel Belin use an antique oak *cassapanca* in their living room, not only for storage but also as a side table.

A seventeenth-century oak chest, or cassapanca, *acts as storage as well as a base for a set of modern vases in Kate Ganz and Daniel Belin's home in Umbria.*

CARVING OUT SPACE

The Niche

One of the benefits of having 2-feet-thick (60-cm) walls is the possibility of digging into them to create niches. In fact, many farmhouses in Italy have small- to medium-size niches in the living areas as well as in the animal stalls. Acting as built-in shelves, niches were used to store anything from cooking utensils to animal feed. It is fun to take advantage of these quirky spaces, or to create new ones. If the niche is large enough, shelves can hold a collection of books. Mount a door on the front, and the entire niche becomes a shallow closet.

Existing niches in these thick Tuscan walls are given a modern look with saturated colors.

Found Spaces

Building codes in Italy are very strict, and space for a restoration is limited to the original footprint of the farmhouse. Since no space can be added, people make use of every bit available, especially when it comes to storage. One of the charms of working with an existing Italian farmhouse is adapting to architectural constraints, which can lead to some very creative—and thoroughly Italian—solutions. Even if you are building a house from scratch or restoring a home outside Italy, some of the more original solutions from farmhouse restorations are worth using. If space is an issue when adapting an existing structure, all the more reason to look to farmhouse restorations for carving out storage space where you thought none existed.

Above: *When Ilaria Miani decided to turn a ground-floor stall into an eat-in kitchen and dining room, she realized that the brick archway separating the two rooms was a bit too low to use as a passage. Instead of closing it up, she used it as a frame for open shelving between the two rooms.*
Opposite: *Kate Ganz and Daniel Belin decided to retain the floor plan of the old animal stall that became their kitchen in Umbria. They turned an awkward corner space near the stairs into a kitchen cupboard by sealing it off with an antique door.*

Opposite: Buildings in Italy can go through many renovations. Doors that once led from one room to the next are closed off, while new entries are opened. A typical solution to a sealed doorway is in Dan Blagg and Francesco Bianchini's town house in Todi. A door that used to lead from the kitchen to another room was closed off when that room became a guest suite. The resulting space between the walls didn't go to waste, and neither did the door itself. The shallow closet with a glazed door now acts as a built-in vitrine for a collection of flea market finds. **Left:** The antique chest in Laura Evan's home in Umbria does double duty as a side table, supporting a lamp and ceramics, and as a storage unit for heavy blankets and quilts that come out each winter. **Right:** "I'm always collecting antique doors," says Ilaria Miani. "So when I see an odd space that would otherwise go unused, I see it as an opportunity to create a closet." At Casellacce, part of a landing at the top of the stairs was closed off to create a linen closet using a door she found abandoned in the original animal stalls.

Storage on View

When faced with limited space, many homeowners decide to play up storage as a design element, rather than hide it behind closed doors. Firewood becomes a focal point of a room when placed beneath three small arches supporting a fireplace at a home at Castello di Reschio. And a wall of terra-cotta tubular wine-storage cubbies becomes almost sculptural in one corner of a room. "We took a very common system used in wineries," explains Benedikt Bolza. "But by filling the spaces between the holes with white plaster, we were able to create a unique pattern."

*For the farmhouses at the Castello di Reschio Estate, architect Benedikt Bolza carefully considered all the details, including storage elements. **Left:** Firewood storage becomes a base for a fireplace. **Right:** Simple wooden doors become dramatic by their repetition in these hallway closets. **Opposite:** Terra-cotta tubes form a dramatic pattern for storing wine.*

CHAPTER THIRTEEN

✦

GARDENS

✦

The most seductive element of Italian homes is perhaps the most difficult to incorporate into our designs: the setting. When we imagine a wood-shuttered, stone-walled, terra-cotta-roofed home, it is usually inserted into a landscape of rolling hills, vineyards, and golden wheat fields. While we can't hope to re-create central Italy in our backyards, we can borrow some of its landscape design details.

Even though most of us think of gardens as flower-filled, colorful explosions of nature, the traditional Italian garden is actually a study in green. Sixteenth-century architects decided to one-up nature by re-creating it in meticulously designed evergreen shrubs and trees that were shaped by humans to impose order on wilderness. This style is now known as *giardino all'Italiana.*

Previous spread: *A classical concrete urn is planted with geraniums and nasturtiums in the garden at La Foce, in Tuscany.* **Opposite:** *The pergola at the Ganz/Belin home in Umbria is covered in wisteria, which provides a thick shade even during the heat of summer. The bases of the pergola's poles are planted with rosemary, while poppies sprout along the edge of the brick paving.*

A perfect example is the gardens at La Foce, an estate in southern Tuscany overlooking the Val d'Orcia. These magnificent gardens were created in the 1920s by the architect Cecil Pinsent for the Origo family, who still own the property. Box hedges are meticulously clipped and divide the garden into "rooms." The horizontal design is punctuated by stately cypresses, which frame the countryside beyond.

*Above: The formal garden at La Foce, in Tuscany, was designed by Cecil Pinsent to complement the property's formal Renaissance villa. Clipped box hedges create a series of garden rooms. **Opposite:** Terra-cotta pots planted with lemon trees are set out in the garden every spring.*

THE LEMON TREE

The climate of central Italy is blazing hot and dry in the summer, but temperatures can sink below freezing in the winter. While myriad plants are hardy enough to survive these extremes, one type needs special protection: the lemon tree, or *albero di limone*. So enamored are Italians of having at least one lemon tree that they are willing to drag it out in the summer and drag it back inside during the winter for shelter. While most farmers make do with a tree or two, grander villas often had rows of yellow-orbed lemon trees set out in heavy handmade terra-cotta pots. This practice gave rise to the construction of *limonaia*, greenhouses set up specifically to protect—and allow one to enjoy—lemon trees during the winter.

CREATING AN ITALIAN GARDEN

Keeping your planting scheme green, and manicured, is a good way to re-create a *giardino all'Italiana* in your own backyard. Framing vistas with carefully placed hedges and bordering annual beds with rows of green perennials bring at least some of the Italian spirit. Consider adding some of the following Italian garden features to your outdoor space:

Terra-Cotta Planters

One of the easiest ways to import a bit of Italy into your garden is to buy a terra-cotta planter or two. These handmade vessels are created out of the same peach-hued clay used for floor and roof tiles.

*Opposite: Laura Evan's pool in Umbria is graced by potted lemon trees in the summer. The tender trees are stored in a ventilated garden shed during the cold winter months. **Left:** At La Foce, hand-thrown terracotta pots are planted with brightly colored geraniums, which line up beneath a row of lavender. **Right:** Evans uses hand-crafted terra-cotta planters around an outdoor seating area centered by a majolica-topped wrought iron table. "While the bones of the garden remain the same, the pots allow me to be a bit whimsical, changing plant colors and perfumes from year to year," Evans says.*

BUILDING NOTES: Pergolas

The summer sun in the Italian countryside may be one of its greatest attractions. But the brutal heat of the midday sun necessitates shade. While most of us envision pergolas as green, leafy arbors covered in vines, remember that the vines need a sturdy structural base.

Pergola design often depends on the materials at hand. The vertical elements can be built of masonry, brick, or wood. The horizontal beams that span the structure are almost always wood. Although sometimes freestanding, most pergolas are constructed so that one side is supported by the walls of the house, creating an outdoor room that becomes an extension of the building.

*Left: Wide chestnut beams support a framework of large and smaller beams, which is topped by a bamboo mat. **Center:** Beams are constructed of sturdy brick, which support the heavy roof made out of wood and terra-cotta tile. This system not only provides total shade, but also protects from rain. **Right:** Stone pilasters support chestnut beams, which are sunk into the wall of the building, supporting the bamboo mat above.*

Shade from the Sun

One of the great joys of Italian life is the possibility of dining *al fresco*. While soft breezes might blow, there is also the blazing sun to confront. Italians are masters at creating ways to tame the heat and filter the light to dapple on lushly set tables.

Pergolas can act as extensions of the house, providing extra rooms to use when weather permits. For this reason, they are often constructed with one side attached to the house itself.

Laura Evans constructed a freestanding pergola of chestnut logs that stands in the area between her swimming pool and merlot-filled vineyard. "I like the fact that it is rather far away from the house," she says. "It makes you feel as if you are really in the middle of nature, since we have such fantastic views from all four sides."

Nature can also help provide shade. We carefully preserved an existing elm tree to form a shady area at our pool's edge. But not everyone is blessed with existing trees, especially when building from scratch. Evans was so enamored of the tradition of planting shade trees that she embraced patience and placed a pair of mulberry trees in front of her brick terrace.

An ancient oak tree provides natural shade at Ilaria and Giorgio Miani's home in Tuscany.

Left: At Gonzola, in Tuscany, chestnut beams support the wisteria-laden pergola on one side, while the other side is supported by the walls of the kitchen. *Right:* Kate Ganz and Daniel Belin chose a similar solution. As at Gonzola, wisteria runs up the poles and frames the landscape. Cane matting provides a filtered shade.

Left: Ilaria Miani was lucky enough to have a century-old oak tree on the grounds of Palazzolaccio. *The full canopy is large enough to shade a garden table set for fourteen.* **Right:** *Laura Evans chose climbing jasmine to cover her freestanding pergola in Umbria. "Even though the vines are slow growing, I decided that it was worth the wait to enjoy the heavenly perfume," says Evans.*

Outdoor Rooms

Most people think of stone-paved courtyards as urban devices, such as those in the *palazzi* of Rome and Florence. But farmhouses had courtyards—known as *cortile* or *corte*—too, though more roughly designed ones. In fact, the term *animale di cortile*, or courtyard animals, refers to small farm animals, such as chickens and rabbits, kept by farmers in semisheltered, enclosed areas created between or next to the main buildings.

Ilaria Miani always tries to design a courtyard of some sort in her home renovations. "A courtyard is the perfect place to relax outside, since it allows you to create microclimates that can adjust to variations in the weather," she explains. "One area can be protected from the wind, another is shady and cool. I also try to create some sort of outdoor kitchen area for baking and grilling." Meanwhile, these spaces also protect delicate plants, such as citrus trees, from heat and cold.

Above: *The courtyard at Palazzolaccio, the Mianis' home in Tuscany, provides a sheltered and shady corner to eat, cook, or just relax.*

Water Features

The Tuscan landscape remains pristine thanks to strict building laws, which often prohibit new pools, which would blot the landscape. Yet water was always an essential part of life on the farm. Preciously hoarded water was collected in open cisterns, reservoirs surrounded by a wall 2 to 3 feet (60–90 cm) high. The water in these containers appeared dark, since the interiors were usually covered in stone, brick, or cement. In fact, the water was dark enough to reflect the sky and remain relatively unobtrusive on the landscape, since it looked like a small pond.

Many homeowners get around building restrictions in Tuscany by creating pools that echo the design of ancient cisterns. Water tanks for farms were simple, usually made of concrete and filled with water. The pools, which mimic these rustic troughs, try to capture their dark, cool look. A dark finish, in shades of gray or green, has the same effect. Finishes include painted surfaces or mosaic.

Left: At Gonzola, on the La Foce estate in Tuscany, the gray stone border of the pool is stepped up to mimic the original water cisterns of Italian farmhouses. Right: The pool at Palazzo Terranova was paved in a mosaic whose colors mimic that of a natural pond. Overleaf: The endless pool at the Mianis' home, Palazzolaccio, has a minimal stone boarder on three sides and overlooks the dramatic Tuscan landscape.

Cooking Outside

For me Italy is two things: spending as much time as possible outside and enjoying and preparing wonderful food. These two aspects of Italian living come together in perfect harmony when you are able to cook outside. Traditionally, most farmhouses had some sort of cooking setup outside. Although the main fireplace in the house was also used for cooking—particularly in the winter—ovens (especially before the introduction of the wood-fueled *cucina economica*) were always outside.

What we think of today as a wood-burning pizza oven was typically the only oven available in a farmhouse. These were often freestanding, although sometimes they were built into the ground floor of the house.

Today it is very easy to install a pizza oven, since the domed cooking chamber is prefabricated. This heat-resistant structure comes in several sizes. The dome is set into a brick surround that looks like a small building.

One of the most wonderful smells in the world has to be food grilling over an open wood fire. Most Italians wouldn't think of using charcoal or gas-fueled grills. "This is one of the most important areas of any house I build," says Ilaria Miani. "It's easy to incorporate, since you just have to have a surface that is flat and deep enough to be able to both build a fire and pull out the embers to cook over." At Palazzolaccio, the grill is 4 feet (122 cm) deep. The large wooden logs burn in a wrought-iron cradle, and the embers fall through and are scooped up and brought forward. A grill, placed over the burning coals, holds the food to be cooked.

Opposite: The outdoor grilling area at Palazzolaccio, the Mianis' home in Tuscany, is located in one corner of a sheltered courtyard, so that grilling can go on all year, rain or shine. **Above:** The pizza oven at Laura Evan's house is a freestanding structure located just a few yards from her kitchen. The oven is a prefabricated element, incorporated by masons into the small brick building.

TERRA-COTTA POTS | FRATELLI BERTI

RIPABIANCA, UMBRIA

Deruta, in Umbria, is well known for its brightly painted tableware. Less well known is the next town down the road: the small hamlet of Ripabianca. A handful of families have been making terra-cotta planters and other vessels there for centuries. Fratelli Berti is located right off the main road, and is well known for its hand-thrown terra-cotta garden planters. Brothers Carlo and Remo, along with Carlo's sons, Eugenio and Francesco, mold clay into massive urns, vases, and planters. Eugenio, arms covered to the elbows in wet, gray clay, gestures to the immense kiln his father Carlo is unloading. "We only recently switched to electricity," he says. "Up until about twelve years ago we still used the old wood ovens. Other than that, everything is still pretty much the same as it was for the last two centuries."

One of their specialties remains immense urns—over 5 feet (1.5 m) high. Once used to store oil and grain, they are now used to decorate homes and gardens. "We

Left: Eugenio Berti carefully works the wet clay on a wheel to form what will be a large terra-cotta planter. Right: With one hand inside the pot and the other on the outside, Eugenio pulls the wet clay both up and out, adjusting his hands as he spins the wheel.

don't know exactly how long our family has been making these," says Carlo. "But we recently found an urn with our family's stamp on it with the date 1835!" The urns are always available with the Fratelli Berti stamp, or can be special-ordered with your own family's crest emblazoned on the front.

The clay comes from Umbria and also from Tuscany, near Sansepolcro. Once formed, the pots are set out in a shaded area so that they don't dry out too fast. The moisture has to be carefully monitored on the large items to avoid cracking. Once cured, the pieces are rolled into the enormous electric kiln for a firing that takes up to twenty-four hours. After firing, the creations are left in the kiln to cool off gently. Once finished, they are quite sturdy and are piled one atop another in the yard, waiting to be shipped throughout Italy and the world.

Left: The finished pot is then cut from the wheel, and left to dry slowly until it is loaded into the kiln to bake. Right: Piles of peach-hued pots are piled haphazardly in the Bertis' outdoor showroom.

BRINGING IT HOME: In the Garden

Bringing a bit of Italy into your own personal landscape doesn't have to involve digging up your backyard and going shopping for trees. Consider a few hand-thrown terra-cotta planters, which are widely imported (see resources, page 228). When filling your pots, think Italian at least in terms of plants. If your climate permits, nothing is more authentic than a classic lemon tree. To create a mini *giardino all'italiana,* line up several rectangular pots along the edge of your patio and plant them with neatly trimmed box hedge.

Dining in dappled shade on a sunny Sunday afternoon is Italian perfection. You can re-create this experience in your own backyard. If you can't build a masonry pergola, consider installing a prefabricated one. Many firms offer kits in either cedar or wrought iron. Another more modern, slightly less rustic but no less Italian option is a large white canvas market umbrella.

Above: *Terra-cotta is used for both the edging of the pool, as well as the geranium-filled containers at Chiarentana on the La Foce estate in Tuscany.* **Opposite:** *Grapevines and an oak tree provide shade over the pergola at Zingoni, the Mianis' home in Tuscany.*

GLOSSARY

affresco: fresco, the technique of painting on wet plaster

albero di limone: lemon tree

al fresco: taking place outside, usually referring to dining

americana: special trowel used for colletta application

animali da cortile: literally "courtyard animals," small farm animals, such as rabbits and chickens, historically kept in the farm's courtyard

armadio: armoire

artigiano: artisan

bagno: bathroom

battiscopa: baseboard

calce: lime

camino: fireplace

cantina: cellar

casa colonica: farmhouse

cascina: country house

cassapanca: wooden storage chest

castagno: chestnut wood

cazzuola: trowel

cera d'api: beeswax

chianche: stone from Trani, in Puglia

colletta: thin secondary layer of plaster on a wall

coppi: curved terra-cotta roof tiles

correnti: transverse beams

corrimano: stair railing

cortile: courtyard

cucina: kitchen

cucina economica: literally "economical kitchen," a cast-iron stove, which burned much more efficiently than a fireplace

falegname: carpenter, cabinetmaker

ferro: iron

ferro battuto: wrought iron

finto fresco: technique of painting on dry plaster, to resemble true fresco

fornace: term used to describe a ceramics company; literally "furnace," referencing the kiln used to make tile

forno: oven

giardino: garden

giardino all'Italiana: an Italian-style topiary garden

gomma lacca: seed lac, a natural shellac

gradino: step

grassello: plaster

grassello di calce: lime plaster

intonaco: plaster

intonaco civile: smooth finishing plaster layer

limonaia: greenhouse used for citrus plants, most commonly lemon trees

loggia: portico

madia: rustic kitchen furniture used to store bread and flour

majolica: tin-glazed earthenware

malenpeggio: two-sided hammer used by stonemasons

marmo: marble

mattone: brick

mattone refrattario: refractory brick or firebrick

mattonelle: tiles, or small bricks

mattone a visa: exposed brick

mercantile: large exterior entry doors used on farmhouse ground floors

olio di lino: linseed oil

olmo: elm

persiana: type of louvered shutter

pietra serena: gray stone from Tuscany

pioppo: poplar

porta: door

portone: second-floor entrance door to a rustic building, accessible via an outside staircase

pozzolana: type of volcanic sand used in creating certain decorative finishing plasters

ringhiera: balcony railing

rinzaffo: preliminary layer of plaster

rovere: oak

rubinetto: tap

scala: stair, staircase

scuri: internal window shutters used to block out light

stucco: final layer of plaster on a wall

stucco romano: type of decorative finishing plaster

stucco veneziano: type of decorative finishing plaster

tavola: wood board

tegola: roof tile

telaio: window frame

testa di moro: a traditional Italian color appearing black with a slight tinge of brown

trave: large supportive beam that spans the room

travertino: travertine stone

*travertino di **Rapolano:*** honey-colored travertine stone from the town of Rapolano or Tivoli

travetti: small squared crossbeams

velo: one of the last layers of plaster on a wall

volta a folio: method of tile laying in which tiles are laid with the edges against one another

voltine: a type of ceiling support developed in places where wood is not plentiful

RESOURCES

ARCHITECTS
AND DESIGNERS
AGG—Steve Arnn
San Francisco, CA
T 415 863 3493
www.agg-design.com

Sarah Bradpiece
SarahBradpiece@gmail.com
(home on pages 2, 7, 89, 95, 198)

Luca Francia
Val di Pierle 58
52044-Cortona AR
Italy
T +39 075 927 3589 /
    +39 0575 619 358
www.terzodidanciano.it/
lucafrancia.html
(homes on pages 1–4, 7, 42, 48,
58–60, 62–63, 67, 77, 82, 89,
95, 97, 102, 123, 128, 130,
157–58, 160, 164, 178, 186–88,
191, 198)

Heidi James
JamesGreenberg Interior Design
33 East 58th Street
Suite 704
New York, NY 10022
T 212 751 2612
F 212 751 2642
www.jamesgreenberg.com

KAA Design Group
Los Angeles, CA
T 310 821 1400
www.kaadesigngroup.com

Ilaria Miani
Interior Design and Furniture
Via Monserrato 35
00186-Roma Italy
T +39 06 683 3160
F +39 683 902172
www.ilariamiani.it
(homes on pages 16–17, 23,
31–32, 61–62, 66, 78, 86, 90,
95–97, 122, 147, 156, 164,
175–76, 182, 189–90, 205,
207–08, 210, 212, 217)

Michael G. Imber Architects
San Antonio, TX
T 210 824 7703
www.michaelgimber.com

Landry Design Group
Los Angeles, CA
T 310 444 1404
www.landrydesigngroup.com

Domenico Minchilli
Vicolo De' Catinari, 3
00186-Roma Italy
T +39 06 683 2206
www.domenicominchilli.com
domenico@minchilli.191.it
(homes on pages 106, 120,
142–44, 154–55, 165, 168)

Mohon Imber Interiors
San Antonio, TX
T 210 828 2194
www.mohon-imber.com

Taylor Lombardo Architects
San Francisco, CA
T 415 433 7777
www.taylorlombardo.com

Timothy D. Osborne
The Organic Gardener
T 718 243 9095
www.theorganicgardenernyc.com

Tucker & Marks Design Inc.
San Francisco, CA
T 415 445 6789
www.tuckerandmarks.com

Walker & Moody Architects
San Francisco, CA
T 415 885 0800
www.walkermoody.com

Chapter 1: Stone Walls
ORGANIZATIONS
Dry Stone Walling Association
of Great Britain
www.dswa.org.uk
(Referrals to stonemasons around
the world, including the U.S.)

COMPANIES / ARTISANS
Drummond Masonry
4540 Cherryvale Avenue
Soquel, CA 95073-9748
T 831 393 1300
F 831 476 3641

Brian Fairfield, Stone Work
PO Box 1412
Kennebunkport, ME 04046
T 207 229 9992
thatstoneguy@yahoo.com

Dan Snow
526 Stickney Brook Road
Dummerston, VT 05301
T 802 254 2673
teatime@together.net
(author of *Listening to Stone* and
In the Company of Stone)

The Stone Foundation
116 Lovato Lane
Santa Fe, NM 87505
T 505 989 4644
www.stonefoundation.org
(U.S.-based organization of
traditional stonemasons)

Michael Weitzner
Thistle Stone Works
340 Goodenough Road
Brattleboro, VT 05301-8967
T 802 254 9869
thistle.stone.works@comcast.net

Chapter 2: Interior Wall Finishes
ORGANIZATIONS
Professional Decorative Painters
Association
www.pdpa.org
(Supplies referrals to decorative
painters and artists across the
U.S.)

COMPANIES / ARTISANS
Adobe Limewash
T 505 897 6767
www.adobelimewash.com

Architectural Coatings +
Design Center
18424 Ventura Boulevard
Tarzana, CA 91356
T 818 757 3900
F 818 757 3937
www.acplusdc.com

Art In Construction
55 Washington Street, #653
Brooklyn, New York 11201
T 718 222 3874 / 212 352 3019
F 718 222 3899 / 212 989 4902
www.design-site.net/aic1.htm
Stephen E. Balser, President

Dolci
T +39 045 800 7126
www.dolcicolor.it
info@dolcicolor.it

The Earth Pigments Company
Cortaro, AZ
T 520 682 8928
www.earthpigments.com

Francesca's Paints Ltd.
34 Battersea Business Centre
99/109 Lavender Hill
London SW11 5QL
UK
T/F 020 7228 7694
www.francescaspaint.com

Fresco Decorative Painting Inc.
324 Lafayette Street, 5th Fl
New York, NY 10012
T 212 966 0676
F 212 966 0756
agnes@frescodeco.com

Frey Plastering Inc.
Novato, CA
www.freyplastering.com
T 415 897 4510

Klein Plastering
PO Box 1008
St. Helena, CA 94574
T 707 963 1227

JJ Snyder Studio
101 Clinton Avenue
Brooklyn, NY 11205
T 347 678 5009
F 718 855 2513
www.jjsnyderstudio.com

Marmorino Venetian Plasters
819 Yonkers Ave
Lower Level
Yonkers, NY 10704
T 914 760 1119
F 914 457 4420
www.stuccolustre.com

Portola Paints
12442 Moorpark Street
Studio City, CA 91604
T 818 623 9053
www.portolapaints.com

Safra Colors
www.safracolors.it

Chapter 3: Floors
TILE FLOORS
Exquisite Surfaces
11817 Wicks Street
Sun Valley, CA 91352
T 818 767 2700
F 818 767 2722
www.xsurfaces.com

Farnese
2211 Alameda Street
San Francisco, CA 94103
www.farnese.info
T 213 655 1819

Fornace Giuliani
Strada ex Aeroporto
05014-Castel Viscardo, TR Italy
T/F +39 0763 361 637
info@fornacigiuliani.it

Paris Ceramics
150 East 58th Street, 7th Fl
New York, NY 10155
T 212 644 2782
F 212 644 2785
www.parisceramics.com

Soli USA
Architectural Surfaces
32 Northeast 39th Street
Miami, FL 33137
T 305 573 4860
F 305 573 9876
www.soliusa.com

Tuscan Resource
T 800 761 1877 / 650 325 7291
www.tuscanresource.com

Walker Zanger
Tile & Stone Showroom
37 E 20th Street
New York, NY 10003
T 212 844 3000
www.walkerzanger.com

WOOD FLOORS
Bois Chamois
411 Kimberly Road
Hockessin, DE 19707
T 302 239 3800 /
800 823 0898
F 302 239 0491
www.boischamois.com

Exquisite Surfaces
11817 Wicks Street
Sun Valley, CA 91352
T 818 767 2700
F 818 767 2722
www.xsurfaces.com

First, Last & Always
1311 22nd Street
San Francisco, CA 94107
T 415 753 8627
F 415 550 2612
www.first_last_always.com

I.J. Peiser's Sons, Inc.
1891 Park Avenue
New York, NY 10035
T 212 348 7500
F 212 348 2323
www.ijpeiser.com
(one of the oldest wood floor
sources in New York)

Listone Giordano
Margaritelli USA Inc.
928 West Chestnut Street
Brockton, MA 02301
T 508 408 4170
F 508 408 4163
www.listonegiordano.com/usa

Pioneer Millworks
1180 Commercial Drive
Farmington, NY 14425
T 800 951 9663 /
585 924 9970
F 585 924 9962
www.pioneermillworks.com

Sutherland Welles Limited
PO Box 180
North Hyde Park, VT 05665
www.sutherlandwelles.com
(polymerized tung oils)

The Vintage Wood Floor
Company
3189 Redhill Avenue, Unit B
Costa Mesa, CA 92626
T 714 646 6861
www.vintagewoodfloors.com

Chapter 4: Ceilings
Pioneer Millworks
1180 Commercial Drive
Farmington, NY 14425
T 800 951 9663
T 585 924 9970
F 585 924 9962
www.pioneermillworks.com

Tuscan Resource
T 800 761 1877 / 650 325 7291
www.tuscanresource.com

Chapter 5: Roofs
Black's Farmwood
PO Box 2836
San Rafael, CA 94912
T 877 321 wood / 415 454 8312
F 415 454 8393
www.blacksfarmwood.com

S. Anselmo
Via Tolomei 61
35010-Loreggia, PD
Italy
T +049 930 4711
F +049 579 1010
www.santanselmo.com

Tuscan Resource
T 800 761 1877 / 650 325 7291
www.tuscanrooftiles.com

Vintage Timberworks, Inc.
47100 Rainbow Canyon Road
Temecula, CA 92592
T 951 695 1003
F 951 695 9003
www.vintagetimber.com

Fratelli Berti
Via dei Mille, 5
06053-Ripabianca, PG
Italy
T +075 973 273

Chapter 6: Windows
Americana
PO Box 322
Avondale Estates, GA 30002
T 800 269 5697
  404 377 0306
F 404 377 1120
www.shutterblinds.com
(wooden shutters)

Blindtek of New York, Inc.
50 North Harrison Avenue,
Suite 17
Congers, NY 10920
T 845 267 8513
F 845 267 8543
www.blindtek.com

Brothers' Windows & Doors
360 Industrial Road, Unit C
San Carlos, CA 94070
T 650 592 9504
F 650 592 9523
www.brotherswindows.com

Reilly Wood Works
Reilly Windows & Doors
901 Burman Blvd.
Building 701
Calverton, NY 11933
T 631 208 0710
F 631 208 0711
www.reillywoodworks.com

The Shutter Mill, Inc.
8517 South Perkins Road
Stillwater, OK 74074
T 405 377 6455
F 405 377 1010
www.kirtz.com

Chapter 7: Doors
Old World Door
Bakersfield, CA
T 661 588 7700 /
  619 819 2575
F 661 244 4477
www.oldworlddoor.com

Pella Window and Doors
Pella Corporation
Customer Service Department
102 Main Street
Pella, IA 50219
T 800 374 4758
www.pella.com

Portera
Pasadena, CA
T 626 639 2130
www.porteradoors.com

Porte del Passato di Enzo Belli
Via Sfrilli, 35
06018-Pistrino, Citerna PG
Italy
www.portedelpassato.com
(antique doors as well as new
ones of salvaged wood)

Tuscan Resource
T 800 761 1877 /
650 325 7291
www.tuscanresource.com
(reclaimed Italian wooden doors)

United House Wrecking
535 Hope Street
Stamford, CT 06906-1300
T 203 348 5371
www.unitedhousewrecking.com

Chapter 8: Fireplaces
Elizabeth Street Gallery
209 Elizabeth Street
New York, NY 10012-4205
T 212 941 4800
www.elizabethstreetgallery.com

Exquisite Surfaces
11817 Wicks Street
Sun Valley, CA 91352
T 818 767 2700
F 818 767 2722
www.xsurfaces.com

Lacole
F.lli Radicchi
Via Aretina, 28
Località Lerchi-Vignone
06012-Citta' di Castello PG
Italy
www.lacole.it

SMC Stone Importer
Distributor & Fabricator
640 Morgan Avenue
Brooklyn, NY 11222
T 718 599 2999
F 718 599 3111
www.smcstone.com

Tuscan Resource
T 800 761 1877 /
650 325 7291
www.tuscanresource.com

United House Wrecking
535 Hope Street
Stamford, CT 06906-1300
T 203 348 5371
www.unitedhousewrecking.com

Chapter 9: Staircases
Fable Inc.
595 Quarry Road
San Carlos, CA 94070
T 650 598 9616
F 650 598 9724
www.fableinc.com

Mariotti
Via Tiburtina, 287
00011-Tivoli Terme RM
Italy
T +39 0774 376 137
F +39 0774 375 298
www.mariottisavema.com

Old World Elegance
Camarillo, CA
T 805 766 1917
F 805 512 8103
www.oldworldelegance.net

SMC Stone Importer Distributor
& Fabricator
640 Morgan Avenue
Brooklyn, NY 11222
T 718 599 2999
F 718 599 3111
www.smcstone.com

Vaselli Marmi
Località Sentino
53040 Rapolano Terme SI
Italy
T +39 0577 7041
F +39 0577 7046
www.vasellimarmi.it/eng

Chapter 10: Kitchens
*Your best source for qualified cabinet
millwork is through an architect or
interior designer. However, these
companies and artisans come highly
recommended:*

Chelsea Kitchen and Bath
325 W 16th Street
New York, NY
T 212 243 5020
www.chelseadesignstudio.net

C. Robert Huggins
50 Cottontail Drive
Portsmouth, RI 02871
T 401 849 7679

Mead & Josipovich Cabinet
Millwork
140 58th Street
Brooklyn, NY 11220
T 718 492 7373

OMA Tech Ltd.
Peter McLaren
14 Boone Street
Yonkers, NY 10704
T 914 494 3860

Rocky Mountain Hardware
Hailey, ID
T 208 788 2013
www.rockymountainhardware.
com

Chapter 11: Bathrooms
GENERAL
Blackman Plumbing Supply
120 Hicksville Road
Bethpage, NY 11714
T 516 579 2000
NYC Showroom:
85 Fifth Avenue, 2nd floor
New York, NY 10003
T 212 337 1000
www.blackman.com

PLUMBING FIXTURES
Aquaware America
www.aquawareamerica.com

Kraft Hardware
315 E 62nd Street
New York, NY 10065

T 212 838 2214
www.kraft-hardware.com

SMC Asia International Co., Inc.
640 Morgan Avenue
Brooklyn, NY 11222
T 718 599 2999
F 718 599 3111
www.smcstone.com

Sonoma Forge
T 800 330 5553
www.sonomaforge.com

Urban Archaeology
143 Franklin Street
New York, NY 10013
T 212 431 4646
F 212 925 3917
www.urbanarchaeology.com

Chapter 12: Storage
Round Trip Imports
33071 W. 83rd Street
De Soto, KS 66018
T 913 583 1511
www.roundtripimports.net

Sonoma Country Antiques
23999 Arnold Drive (Hwy 121)
Sonoma, CA 95476
T 707 938 8315
F 707 938 0134
www.sonomaantiques.com

Chapter 13: Gardens
Cedar Store
T 888 293 2339
F 724 444 5301
www.cedarstore.com

Chelsea Garden Center Inc.
580 11th Avenue
New York, NY 10036
T 212 727 7100 /
    212 929 2477
F 212 727 3637
www.chelseagardencenter.com

Collezione
Menlo Park, CA
T 650 327 1342
F 650 462 0706
www.collezioneusa.com

Elizabeth Street Gallery
209 Elizabeth Street
New York, NY 10012-4205
T 212 941 4800
www.elizabethstreetgallery.com
Forno Bravo
www.fornobravo.com
(Tuscan wood-burning pizza
ovens and terra-cotta planters)

Marston Langinger
T 212 575 0554
www.marston-and-langinger.com
(greenhouses and orangeries)

Proler Garden Antiques
Los Angeles, CA
T 310 683 0868
F 310 459 2577
www.garden-antiques.com

The Shade Experts
T 561 422 3200
www.theshadeexperts.com

Tuscany 2 You
17842 Irvine Blvd., #132
Tustin, CA 92780
T 714 277 3812
F 714 730 4055
www.tuscany2you.com

Places mentioned or
photographed in this book

Castello di Reschio
Fattoria di Reschio
06060 Lisciano Niccone PG
Italy
T +39 075 844 362
F +39 075 844 363
www.reschio.com
(pages 148–149, 167, 170, 181,
194–95)

Fattoria di San Martino
Via Martiena, 3
53045-Montepulciano SI
Italy
T/F +39 0578 717463
www.fattoriasanmartino.it
(pages 18, 21, 23, 27, 36, 43, 45,
47, 63, 136, 189)

La Foce
Strada della Vittoria, 61
53042 Chianciano Terme, SI
Italy
T/F +39 057 869 101
www.lafoce.com
(pages 13, 20, 64, 94, 128, 138,
179, 196, 200, 201, 206, 216)

Fornace Giuliani
Strada ex Aeroporto
05014-Castel Viscardo, TR
Italy
T/F +39 0763 361 637
www.fornacigiuliani.it
(pages 41, 49–53)

Fratelli Berti
Ripabianca
Berti Carlo E Remo S.n.c.
Terrecotte
Via Mille, 5
06053-Deruta PG
Italy
T +075 973 139
(pages 81, 214–15)

Gualtiero Brunelli
Via Piana, 178
06050-Pantalla di Todi PG
Italy
T +39 075888176
(page 100)

Lacole
F.lli Radicchi
Via Aretina 28
Località Lerchi-Vignone
06012-Città di Castello PG
Italy
www.lacole.it
(pages 48, 74, 131–32, 180)

La Locanda del Loggiato
Bed & Breakfast
Piazza del Moretto 30
53027-Bagno Vignoni SI
Italy
T +39 0577 888925
www.loggiato.it
(pages 24, 34, 46, 56, 84, 103,
119, 127, 178, 184)

Laura Evans Homes
www.poderecalzone.com
(pages 10, 40, 141, 150, 174, 179,
193, 202–3, 207, 213)

Miani Homes in Tuscany
(Includes Caselacce,
Palazzolaccio, Zingoni)
Giorgio Miani
giorgiomiani@tin.it
(pages 16–17, 23, 31–32, 61–62,
66, 78, 86, 90, 95–97, 122, 147,
156, 164, 175–76, 182, 189–90,
205, 207–8, 210, 212, 217)

Legnami Nucciarelli
Colle di Sopra, 19
Castell'ottieri GR
Italy
T/F +39 0564 633 150
www.legnaminucciarelli.com
(page 65)

Palazzo Terranova
Località. Ronti
06010-Morra PG
Italy
T +39 075 857 0083
www.palazzoterranova.com
(pages viii, 30, 54, 111, 134, 145,
173, 209)

Porte del Passato di Enzo Belli
Via Sfrilli, 35
Pistrino, Citerna PG
Italy
www.portedelpassato.com
(pages 104, 112–13, 116–18)

Tenuta Santa Croce
Mignianella dei Marchesi, 597
06019-Umbertide PG
Italy
T +075 941 1564
www.santacroce.de
(pages 92, 101, 109, 176)

Vaselli Marmi
Località. Sentino
53040-Rapolano Terme SI
Italy
T +39 0577 7041
F +39 0577 7046
(pages 148–49)

ACKNOWLEDGMENTS

I would like to thank those who graciously opened their doors and allowed us to feature their homes. The beauty within these pages is due to your generosity. Thank you Kate Ganz, Daniel Belin, Dan Blagg, Francesco Bianchini, the Carabba family, Ilaria and Giorgio Miani, Peter and Maria Theresa von Magnis in Rehder, Laura Evans, Carolyn and James Twist, Karin Lijftogt, Antonio Giorgini, Evgeny Lebedev, Donata Origo, Benedetta Origo, Sabrina and Barbara Marini, and the Bolza family.

It was a pleasure and an honor to explore the techniques, crafts, and skills that the following artisans keep alive: Fratelli Berti, Enzo Belli and Family, Fornace Giuliani, Legnami Nucciarelli, Vaselli Marmi, and the Brunelli family.

A special thanks to the people who kindly hosted Simon on his travels: Laura Evans, Palazzo Terranova, Kate Ganz and Daniel Belin, Fattoria di San Martino, Locanda del Loggiato, and Donata Origo.

A special thanks to architect Luca Francia, who shared invaluable information concerning Kate Ganz and Daniel Belin's home in Umbria. And more thanks to vault expert extraordinaire, and American Academy of Rome Prize winner John Ochsendorf, for explaining the dynamics of vaults. For help in finding excellent sources in the USA, I thank Heidi James at JamesGreenberg Interior Design and Maggie Passarelli Lenconi and Louis Passarelli of Tuscan Resource. And special thanks to Mario Lovergine, for turning Domenico's sketches into legible drawings.

Heartfelt thanks to Ingrid Abramovitch, who arrived at Artisan to find this huge project waiting on her desk. Thank you for your expert editing, which turned the massive amount of information into a coherent and orderly resource. And to Jan Derevjanik and Susan Baldaserini, for sifting through hundreds of photographs and drawings and merging them with the text to make a coherent—and beautiful—whole. And to Erin Sainz, Nancy Murray, Suzanne Lander, and everyone else at Artisan for their patience and hard work.

Thank you to my agent, Betsy Amster, whose sage advice helped this book along. And, of course, infinite thanks to Ann Bramson, who decided the world needed this book, and that I should be the one to write it.

As always, this book owes everything to the extraordinary talent of Simon McBride. His enthusiasm and vision enables this book to sing. But most of all, thanks to my husband Domenico Minchilli, whose knowledge, experience, and love—for both the author and her subject—fill every page.

INDEX

Page numbers in *italics* refer to illustrations.